KU-065-904

VICKERS GROUP ENGINEERING LIMITED

Huw Beynon and Hilary Wainwright

The Workers' Report on Vickers

The Vickers Shop Stewards Combine Committee Report
on Work, Wages, Rationalisation, Closure and Rank-and-File
Organisation in a Multinational Company

Introduction by
the Vickers Shop Stewards Combine Committee

Pluto Press

First published 1979 by Pluto Press Limited
Unit 10 Spencer Court
7 Chalcot Road, London NW1 8LH

Copyright © Pluto Press
ISBN 0 86104 066 X paperback

Designed by Colin Bailey
Cover designed by Terry Seago
Cover photograph of Scotswood works
by Tish Murtha
Cartoons on pages i, 27 and 69
by Bryan McAllister

Photoset by Bristol Typesetting Company Limited
Barton Manor, St Philips, Bristol
Printed and bound in Great Britain at
The Camelot Press Ltd, Southampton

Contents

Preface

This report has been written in association with the Vickers National Shop Stewards Combine Committee. It is termed a 'workers' report' because it is based upon discussions which we have had with workers and shop stewards in many of the Vickers plants operating throughout Britain. These people expressed a concern that a report be put together which demonstrated to them and the other workers in the company the ways in which Vickers Ltd. has changed and how it continues to affect their lives. The combine committee felt that such an account would be useful to them and to 'the labour movement generally'. We hope that they are not disappointed with the result and that they feel it was worth the time and effort they put into it.

The fact that these people felt the need to analyse the structure of the company they work for is not surprising. Giant corporations like Vickers operate on an increasingly multi-plant (and multi-national) basis and follow strategies which cannot be clearly grasped from the experience of just one plant and locality. At ICI and Lucas, in the machine tool industry and in the motor industry, among others, workers and shop stewards have shown a similar interest in 'research' and in developing their own counter-strategies. In this they have had little help from the resources of their union head offices. Instead they have worked closely with research workers in universities, polytechnics and local resource centres. This report is therefore just one example of a more general activity, and we very much hope it will help to strengthen the development of research which bases itself upon the expressed needs and interests of the people who work on the shop floors of offices and factories and experience the consequences of decisions taken by 'experts' and accountants in head offices.

Apart from shop stewards at Vickers a number of people have read various drafts of the report and made helpful comments: Terry Austrin, Dave Bailey, Gary Craig, Bob Davis, Christopher Hird and Mary Kaldor. Others have provided us with useful pieces of information: Martin Legassick on Vickers in South Africa; the Benwell CDP on Vickers in Tyneside and the Labour Research Department on Vickers' accounts. We are thankful to them all. Final thanks to Sheila Shippen and Patricia Bruce who persevered with the typing and retyping and to the SSRC and Durham University who provided the finance and resources to make the report possible.

HB/HW
Durham. October 1978

Introduction

by the officers of the Vickers National Shop Stewards Combine Committee

The city of Newcastle upon Tyne, in which lies one of the old parts of the Vickers empire, is built on and around the remains of earlier empires which invaded the north east coast. Nearing the end of its long journey from the Solway Firth to Wallsend on Tyne, Hadrian's Wall passes below the Literary and Philosophical Society building in the centre of the city. Down the river, Tynemouth Priory – often sacked by the Vikings in their marauding into the ancient kingdom of Northumbria – stands over the river mouth. High above the ancient river-ford is the castle from which the city takes its name, built in about 1100 by William Rufus, son of William the Conqueror, during the last great conquest of these isles.

This book is about the new invaders – the multinational corporations – and the increasing powers that they exercise over our lives. It is also about the organisations that workers are building in response to their growth. This 'new invasion' is, of course, much more subtle than the old: the corporate executive negotiating with the local authority for factory sites replaces the axe-wielding Viking with territorial ambitions; the wages system replaces the forced labour used to build the Roman wall; and public relations officers supplant the brutal techniques used by most invaders to destroy the culture of the conquered population and replace it with their own. The means may be different but the aim is the same – to allow a small number of people to control a much larger number of people and make themselves rich and powerful in the process.

Tyneside saw the beginnings of the industrial revolution founded on the coalfields and iron ore deposits of the area and fuelled by the genius of local engineers – Stephenson, Swan, Armstrong and Parsons. Their relics are still with us in the factories they built and the products they invented, many of which are still being manu-factured, albeit in an improved form. But today the production unit is invariably, part of a world-wide corporation. One of the enduring monuments to Lord Armstrong, the founder of the Newcastle firm which amalgamated with Vickers in 1927, must be the Engineering Employers' Association which he set up in 1896 and which had as its objective 'to protect and defend the interests of employers against combinations of workmen'. The structure of some trade unions today is still largely based on their response to the Victorian industrial entrepreneurs of whom Armstrong was a prime example: the branch based on a geographical area, the district committee and national executive dealing with local and national employers' associations reflect this era.

In contrast the organisations of capitalism have been aggregating at an increasing rate, particularly over the last twenty years. Today less than 100 multinational companies control 75 per cent of the Western world's capital, industrial production and distribution, and dominate world trade and the monetary system. Here in Britain there are over half a million companies, but fewer than 1 per cent of them account for half of Britain's assets, half its output, and half its trade. The top 100 firms in Britain now control over 50 per cent of manufacturing industry. What has been and what is the response of the labour movement to this massive increase in corporate power?

A number of our leaders have taken the classical road out of the struggle and joined the enemy. The list of former Labour cabinet ministers now sitting in the board rooms of the multinational companies is formidable, ranging from Sir Hartley Shawcross of the 1945 Labour government, now with Shell, to Lord Glenamara (Ted Short) who left the present government to join Cable and Wireless, and taking in our own Vickers chairman, Lord Robens. What is a more disturbing development, however, is the increasing incorporation of active trade union officials onto the boards of 'quangos'. These 'quasi-autonomous government organisations' are composed of employer and union representatives and staffed by what are, in effect, civil servants. The old hero of the left in the unions, Hugh Scanlon, is now reputed to earn £5000 a year from his membership of bodies like the National Economic Development Council, the National Enterprise Board, the Gas Board and the Engineering Industry Training Board. This incorporation of our political and industrial leadership into the capitalist system is leaving a vacuum which is being filled by the combine committee, a national and international working class organisation based on the shop stewards committees in the different plants and factories of a multinational company.

Combine committees have had a chequered career within the trade union movement. Owing some inspiration to the syndicalists' ideas of industrial unionism propagated at the beginning of this century, they emerged in some strength in the 1939-45 wartime period and continued afterwards. With the increasing centralisation of policy and decision-making in the large companies shop stewards realise the need for a parallel or 'mirror' organisation on the union side. The shortcomings of existing official channels in meeting the co-ordinated management policies of a company which has plants in many countries makes this need clear. However the official union attitude to combine committees is an ambivalent one. Most research documents on union structure see in the shop stewards' combine committees an effective form of organisation within the multi-national sector (this has been echoed in the Bullock report and the recent government White Paper on industrial democracy with their advocacy of joint representation committees). In practice however (and certainly in our experience), some full time officials are suspicious and even hostile to shop stewards power as expressed in the combine committee. While the proponents of combine com-mittees are clear that these are a necessary addition to existing union structures and not meant to replace them, many officials see them as a threat. The problems facing the growth of the committees are enormous: hostility from the company, some hostility from the union, and a total lack of resources. While the Labour government pumps £11 millions a day into private industry, shop stewards in large companies are often unable to meet regularly because some of their committees can't afford the train fares. What sort of a 'pluralist democracy' is this? The Lucas Shop Stewards Combine Committee produced their corporate plan with no help from the government or the company and with no other resources than their own intelligence and creativity. Yet this document will prove to be one of the watersheds in the socialisation of industry and the development of working class power.

In this 'workers report' we have examined the operation of the multinational company Vickers from the point of view of the shop floor and the communities that the factories are based in and should be serving. We hope that this report will make a contribution to the debate on workers control in industry and also help the growth of combine committees as a first step to industrial democracy and the socialisation of the military-industrial complex. If this happens we will be well satisfied.

J Chequer *Chairman*

P Tolchard *Secretary*

J Murray *Treasurer*

Part 1

VICKERS IN THE CORPORATE WORLD

This report sets out to examine critically (and from the standpoint of the workers' organisation) the operation of a large British engineering company – Vickers Ltd. It begins in part one by outlining the post war history of the company: the financial crisis it experienced and the dramatic changes that have taken place in its organisation and structure. The aim here is to make clear that the Vickers company has changed radically over the past ten years, and also to indicate that these changes have to an important extent been enforced by 'external' financial pressure and have benefited from a close relationship with government.

In many ways the changes that have taken place in Vickers can be seen as an illustration of general changes at work within British society. For this reason the first chapter examines the big business sector of the British economy. Production in this sector is increasingly concentrated in the hands of fewer and fewer giant corporations, and chapter one outlines the strengths of these firms and some of the strategies operated by them. It is against this background that the crisis and re-organisation of Vickers can best be understood.

Chapter 1

The Corporate Economy

On 19 September 1977 the *Guardian* reported that government ministers were enjoying 'a rush of good will last night after their success in capturing Ford's new £180 million engine plant for Britain'. The same article reported the Labour Prime Minister's observation that 'Ford have shown confidence in Britain. In return we must do all we can to justify that confidence by maintaining high productivity and reliability and good industrial relations.'

Callaghan's use of 'we' together with the 'unprecedented level of state assistance' reported by the *Observer* and the muscle which Ford used to get it, says a lot about the present situation. It says even more when we add to it the deal which Chrysler were able to wring out of this same government. It points to the power of multinational corporations: a power which is reflected in the changing nature of the British economy.

Since the war manufacturing production in Britain has become increasingly concentrated in the hands of fewer and fewer massive corporations: corporations which operate from a large number of plants situated in Britain and the rest of the world. In 1950, for example, the top one hundred manufacturing firms in Britain controlled about one fifth of manufacturing output; in 1970 they controlled about one half; the estimate for 1980 is two thirds. In 1950 each one of these firms operated from an average of about 25 plants in Britain; in 1970 the average was 75. In the 1970s, 75 per cent of capital movements in and out of Britain have taken the form of capital transfers within and between multinational corporations.

Reliable estimates indicate that by 1985, 80 per cent of capital assets in the 'non-communist world' will be controlled by two hundred or so large corporations. As it is corporations like General Motors have sales figures which are larger than the national income of South Africa, and a wages bill that exceeds the income of Eire. The average growth rate of the biggest corporations is two or three times that of all Western countries and between them they control something like $200 billion worth of assets.

The tendency is both universal and powerful. In Britain the lives of working people are increasingly coming within the ambit of these corporations. Most industrial workers at one time or another in their lives will be employed by one. On Tyneside the official estimates (which are certainly on the low side) indicate that 54 per cent of the labour force employed in medium-to-large factories work for a multinational corporation. On Merseyside the figure is (or was before the latest round of plant closures) as high as 80 per cent[1].

The implications of these changes were discussed within the Labour Party in the early 1960s, and the 1964 election manifesto, *Signpost for the Sixties*, argued that 'The greatest single problem of modern democracy is how to ensure that the handful of men who control these concentrations of power can be responsive and responsible to the nation'. The problem was stated but never solved – or even acted upon with any degree of resolution. Under successive Labour governments the power of big business in Britain has increased. In this period its presence has played a determining role in British politics (a fact of great irony given the media's portrayal of Jack Jones as 'the most powerful man in Britain'). It has been experienced by working class people through speed-up, redundancy, and the dole queue; mergers, take-overs and rationalisation. It is becoming increasingly clear that the giant corporations plan their operations on a global basis, that the politics of nation-states are being altered by this process, and that workers organisations face radically new problems in advancing the interests of their members and their families in this new period of capitalist development.

From entrepreneur to head office

As the workshop gave way to the factory in the nineteenth century so too, in the twentieth, has the factory and the family firm been replaced by the corporation. Organised first on a national basis, then elaborated through a multi-divisional structure these firms have finally developed on a global scale. This is illustrated in the assessment made of the Massey Ferguson corporation by the

Financial Times: '[it is] a highly professional organisation which has resources and flexibility to determine not only its products but how and in which country they can most profitably be manufactured'.

In this development toward globally-organised production the nineteenth century entrepreneur (the owner-manager who hired, fired, bought and sold – the boss) has been replaced by the *head office* in which executives, accountants and managers plan and organise the detailed growth and development of the corporation. The Ford Motor Company (made up of Ford Europe, Ford Asia, etc.) fronts its main building in Detroit with the sign *Ford: World Headquarters*. It is there that the corporation's investment policy is worked out. 'London' figures in a similar way in the decision-making processes of the British-owned multinationals.

Over the past ten years union officials and shop stewards in Britain have noticed the change. One official of the AUEW in the north-east of England put it like this:

> Over the past ten years there have been tremendous changes. Ten years ago I could go to any one of the engineering plants in the area and feel confident that we could have meaningful negotiations. Today, though, with the multinational corporations, you're negotiating with ghosts. It's no longer plants but groups: Group Personnel and Group Administration with national people making the decisions. I think this is probably worse for officials negotiating with the American companies – because there the ghosts are in Detroit.

Many of the multinational corporations feel vulnerable to these charges of over-centralised decision making. Some of them attempt to offset centralisation with talk of local autonomy and participation. Massey Ferguson's British management insist that 'Things are not controlled from Toronto. The whole philosophy of the corporation is directed towards ensuring the maximum local autonomy.' (*Financial Times*, 17 June 1977). Of course, there are degrees of centralisation, and some companies may foster decentralised decision-making on certain issues. However the position of plants within the overall structure of the firm limits this autonomy. In this context two American commentators have observed that:

> a decentralising ideology masks a centralising reality. The factors which create this situation include an integration of

multinational operations, an increasing speed of technological change, and the rapid development of global techniques, strategies and information collection.[2]

The accounting scheme of things

The corporate centre, overtly or discreetly, operates as a monitoring device within the multinational firm and, most importantly, as the focus of *financial control*. It is here that the information relating to the performance of a particular plant or division, on a particular site in a particular country, is collected, programmed and assessed. This assessment – in the most powerful corporations – is detailed and thorough. Perhaps ITT of all the multinational corporations demonstrates this tendency in its most overt form. Under the chairmanship of Harold S. Geneen control within the corporation has become highly centralised and dominated by accounting criteria. The performance of managers is held regularly to account and it is made clear to them that the yardstick of business is money (profit) and not simply production and employment. As one of them put it: 'If you're responsible for one product like cars or hotels, you get emotionally involved: you get to like them too much.'[3] To this end – breaking the emotional link – managers are moved regularly from one part of the corporation to another, from one side of the world to another.

The Ford Motor Company provides another clear example of the position that an accounting logic of profit and loss plays within the strategy of the giant corporations. Ford executives make no secret of the fact that the company is organised around the rational and aggressive pursuit of profit (something which a recent chief executive termed 'buck smelling'). At Warley in Essex – the headquarters of Ford Europe – senior management are proud of the fact that they can price any part of their cars 'down to four decimal places'. In Detroit, Ford employ a financial analyst whose preoccupation is with international currency movements. He keeps a detailed file on government officials in the countries within which Ford operates: all in an attempt to get 'into the skin of financial bureaucrats'. In this he seems to have been particularly successful, predicting 69 out of the last 75 monetary crises and advising Ford accordingly.[4]

But perhaps the most graphic example of the logic inherent in the company's organisation became public in 1977 when, after seven years of evasion and secrecy, it was clearly established that the company's accounting scheme extended to an evaluation of human life itself. In 1970 Ford had rushed into the 'sub-compact' market in competition with the Volkswagen Beetle. Ford's mini was the Pinto, designed – to save weight – with a fuel tank which straddled the car's rear axle. The company's tests (undertaken after the decision on production had been made and when plants were already tooled up for the Pinto) revealed that the Pinto was vulnerable when involved in a rear-end collision. In short, the car was likely to explode. In spite of this, production went ahead and people burned to death. In arriving at the decision to produce the car Ford's executives went through an extremely clinical appraisal of the situation. They assessed the costs and the benefits involved in redesigning the Pinto. An internal memo from the company read:

Benefits

savings	180 burn deaths
	180 serious burn injuries
	2,100 burned vehicles
unit cost	$200,000 per death
	$67,000 per injury
	$700 per vehicle
total benefit	$180 \times (\$200,000) + 180 \times (\$67,000) + 2,100 \times (\$700)$
	$= \$49.5 \ million$

Costs

sales	11 million cars
	1.5 million light trucks
unit cost	$11 per car
	$11 per truck
total cost	$11 \ million \times (\$11) + 1.5 \ million \times (\$11)$
	$= \$137 \ million$

At the bottom line the cost to Ford far outweighed the benefit to society ('even', to quote from the memo, 'using a number of highly favourable benefit assumptions'). It was the bottom line which decided the issue.[5]

You could say that Ford – in putting a 'dollar value' on human life – 'went too far'. But corporate decision-making daily – if implicitly – places that dollar value on people's lives. A 'cost' and 'benefit' table like the one above is at the back of all major corporate decisions. The closure of a plant, the speed up of an assembly line, the pollution of rivers are all justified by a similar logic. It is a logic of profit, and it was made clear by Dr Heinz Redwood, general manager of corporate planning at Fison's:

> A leading question in the setting of objectives is the relative priority between financial and non-financial objectives. What should managers choose today – social responsibility or earnings per share? Can the primary objective of a publicly quoted company be non-financial? I think not. We are surrounded by voices telling us that it can and must; but I think it cannot and must not. (*Financial Times* 12 April 1977)

Profit drives the modern corporation as powerfully as it did the family firm; in its multinational form, however, capital's desire to accumulate takes on heightened possibilities. While the family firm was dependent on assets fixed in a single locality the modern corporation faces no such constraint.

In planning their investments the men who run the giant corporations operate with something approaching a *global* strategy. In developing this strategy the corporate decision-makers

> co-ordinate decisions on pricing, financial flows, marketing, tax minimisation, research and development, and political intelligence on a global level, and it is this that gives the world corporation its peculiar advantage and extra-ordinary power.[6]

They will exploit the position of low wage and vulnerable work forces; declare most profits in countries whose profit taxes are least punitive, pressure national governments for the most favourable handouts and so on. In all this, it must be said, they have been rather effective.

The role of governments

In Britain the central government provided an average of £11 million worth of aid to business on every day of the year in 1977. Grants, loans, allowances and advance factories are all part of this aid. But it would be wrong to overstress the extent to which the companies in their relationship with national states are governed by the concern to maximise short-run profits. While the flexibility provided by the structure of the multinational corporation does allow investment to be directed from one part of the world to another, the corporations and their accountants benefit from some degree of permanence. Chess players need a board on which to assess and plan the relative advantage of one move over another. In this case the squares are made up of nation states, with national markets, governments, trade unions and labour forces. For this reason company strategies have needed to be more far-reaching and elaborate than the simple *short term* manipulation of their global advantage.

A glimpse of the extent to which this is recognised by business leaders can be gained from a speech entitled 'The Corporation in 1990' which was given by a company chairman at a White House conference in 1972. In his view, by 1990 government and business and labour – in fact all elements of society – should be sitting down to plan the future, to establish national priorities and to agree upon objectives and strategy. 'Planning' has ceased to be a dirty word for big business. The attitude of the giant corporations toward the state is far removed from the 'laissez-faire' approach characteristic of earlier periods of capitalist development. In the post-war period in Europe and America the corporations, while not always the initiators, have tended to encourage rather than resist the in-volvement of government in economic affairs. They have been actively involved in the innumerable state institutions set up to this effect.

In Britain this tendency has been very clear. The hostility directed toward the Labour Party in the inter-war years had changed by 1964 when *The Economist* encouraged its readers to vote

Could you use a piece of Wales?

The whole of Wales is an assisted area and incoming industry qualifies for a wide range of government incentives.

If you could make good use of a piece of Wales, we'd like to hear from you.

Because the Welsh Development Agency offers incoming industry factories, finance and advice.

Complete the coupon and we'll tell you more about the Welsh Development Agency. And about Wales.

Welsh Development Agency, Treforest Industrial Estate, Pontypridd, Mid Glamorgan CF37 5UT. Telephone: Treforest (044 385) 2666. Telex: 497516.

Welsh Development Agency

for Harold Wilson's party as the only one capable of establishing the necessary framework for economic development (state aid to restructure industries, planning and wage regulation). The post-war years have amply borne out the observations made by Aneurin Bevan at the 1944 Labour Party conference. He put it this way:

> In practice it is impossible for the modern state to maintain an independent control over the decisions of big business. When the state extends its control over big business, big business moves in to control the state. The political decisions of the state become so important a part of the business transactions of the combines that it is a law of their survival that most decisions should suit the needs of profit making.[7]

And so it has proved. In a context where economic stability and growth is dependent upon the state regulation of economies, the multinational corporations have been adept at re-fashioning the relationship between 'business' and 'government'. In this their aim has not been to 'keep politics out of business', but rather to make 'business' the very stuff of 'politics'. Requiring a labour force and the political stability which will allow them to plan their figures, the multinationals have been open to a variety of relationships with governments. Suitably arranged (and compensated) nationalisa-governments. The Chrysler Corporation, for example, makes the boast of being the 'most flexible in the world when it comes down to who has what share', and many of the multinationals welcome the prospect of setting up plants in East Europe and China.

One careful study of the strategies followed by big business and the men who run the giant corporations has argued that the 'business view' of the future saw the state fulfilling certain key functions. It was to be:

> the protector of the free movement of capital and goods; a regulator and educator of the labour market; a balancer of the private economy; a consensus builder able at least to ameliorate correctable injustices through . . . social security etc., and a pacifier prepared to deal with the social effects of uncorrectable injustices with force.[8]

In sum, the corporate accountants are looking to national govern-ments for more than merely an economic subsidy. The process is not simply one of 'economic management'. What these accounting brains have adjusted to is the fact that the climate of profit making depends upon the broader social environment, and this too needs to be regulated and constrained. As such they expect that nation-states will also need to act as the 'custodian of the national environment ready to maintain all aspects . . . essential to a good business climate – clean air, drinkable water, good roads, adequate schools, hospitals, communications, waste disposal and above all, a reasonably contented population'.[9]

To point to the corporation's view of things does not make them come true. Neither should it be thought that the corporations are infinitely adaptable or that certain political developments within nation states could not be against their interests.[10] Rather it is to make clear that *national* economies are being radically affected by the presence of corporations which produce on a global basis. Not all economies are affected in the same way, and the role which the multinational corporations play will vary from state to state. In Britain the *centralisation* of power within manufacturing is important. But so is the international vulnerability of key sections of British industry. In this situation the *kind* of policies which have been followed by British governments since the war have also had an important effect. These more complicated aspects of the situation will become clearer when we examine the way in which one British company – Vickers Ltd. – has, over the past twenty years, related to the growth of the corporate economy.

Chapter 2

The Old Vickers: The Government's Gunsmith

Talk to people about Vickers and they think of an old established engineering and armaments firm: a firm that dates back to the nineteenth century; a very 'British' firm. And such an image has much truth in it. For years Vickers occupied a comfortable position as both the privately-owned arsenal of the British state and a powerful monopoly in the international arms market.

Barrow in Furness and Newcastle upon Tyne were built around the ship and gun factories of Vickers and Armstrong. In two world wars people became accustomed to the name.

Cost plus

The historical origin, and strength, of Vickers lay in its role as a government contractor. The security of the company was guaranteed by its monopoly of heavy defence contracts and by the 'cost plus' principle on which all such contracts were priced. This 'cost plus' system not merely ensured that risks and unexpected expenses were covered; it also provided Vickers with an exorbitant rate of profit. In 1943 (following a statement from a southern Vickers shop stewards committee) the Committee of Public Accounts set up an inquiry into the company. It examined the profit rates on contracts for the hull and machinery of warships ordered from Vickers between 1936 and 1939. These contracts covered 32 warships, and at the time 7 per cent was generally considered to be a fair profit on warship construction. The inquiry revealed five cases where profits were between 10 per cent and 20 per cent; nine of profits between 20 per cent and 30 per cent; another nine between 30 per cent and 50 per cent; four where the rate was between 50 per cent and 80 per cent; and one of a profit rate of over 80 per cent. The committee went on to add that their attention had been drawn to a number of cases in which prices certified by the government's technical departments to be 'fair and reasonable' had been 'shown by cost investigations to be excessive.'

As Fenner Brockway explained in 1944 'The officials of His Majesty's technical departments are recruited often from the staffs of private firms, who usually show a most co-operative spirit in releasing them from their employ'.[1] 'Cost plus' was therefore solidified by personal contact and the regular interchange of personnel between government departments and the continuing companies. Vickers relied deeply upon a network of individual contacts and friendships in key positions. A glimpse of what this network meant can be caught in some of the fairly everyday letters written by Sir Charles Craven, managing director of Vickers until 1940. Just before the war he wrote to a president of an American associate company,

> I wonder whether you have heard that our old friend Percy Addison is now the Director of Dockyards. I helped him all I could to get the job . . . It means his retirement, but also it means his having a permanent job for about ten years if he behaves himself, and as he has no private means worth talking about, you will appreciate what this means. I have suggested to him that you and I, he and John (who is anxious to meet you) should have a party and thoroughly wet the appointment next time you are over here.

On another occasion he wrote about a tender to the Admiralty,

> I also think that perhaps it would be worth while putting forward a tender for six boats, the total number to be built. I have had a word with the director of contracts at the Admiralty who is a friend of mine, and who would like this. He I know, tried to get us the order for all five submarines last year.

All this was known within the company as 'the service approach'. It was a style which – coupled with the innumerable ex-officers who ran the company's affairs – branded Vickers as a 'British institution'. Another side of this was illustrated well during the Suez invasion when a Commander Lakin, the managing director of the Vickers Elswick works on Tyneside, took fifty engineering workers with him to Egypt to help maintain army equipment.

This, then, was the 'old Vickers': steelmaker and armaments manufacturer; the producer of guns, tanks, warships and aircraft. Tightly linked – both socially and economically – to governments which provided it with a guaranteed (and lucrative) market. As one shop steward reflected in 1977 'if you couldn't make profits under those conditions you'd commit suicide'.

Vickers was on to a good thing, but it couldn't last for ever. The conditions for 'old Vickers' were closely tied up with the strength of British imperialism. Suez marked the end of that; and Commander Lakin's adventure was to be the last act in the old relationship. The new period of rapid technological change and the growth of international competition from multinational corporations was to prove a testing one for both the British state and for national firms like Vickers. The company was particularly ill-equipped to deal with the new situation. It has survived, but on the way it has experienced a severe financial crisis and (with considerable help from the government) been forced to radically restructure its operations. Before examining these changes – the making of the 'new Vickers' – it will be useful to outline in a bit more detail the extent of the company's vulnerability in the 1960s.

The legacy

Clearly, arms selling is still big business – perhaps bigger now than it ever was. There were fortunes to be made in arms sales in the 1960s and some British companies – like GEC, Lucas and Plessey – made theirs. But not Vickers. There was a clear reason for this. The place of Vickers as an arms dealer of international power was based upon the strength of British heavy and mechanical engineering, a strength that came from that industry's position within the 'first industrial revolution' and the skill and experience of the engineering workers. The profits that Vickers was making in the 1930s rested on the lead which the company had established in the latter part of the nineteenth century. But in those years innovations were taking place in completely new sectors: changes leading to the development of advanced electronic engineering, which would transform the armaments trade. In a sense 'the past', once an advantage of the company and the engineering industry generally, had become its albatross. Shop stewards from some of the older Vickers plants will tell you that 'the machinery in there ought to be in a museum – in fact I don't think a museum would take some of it!'

Survival in the arms trade required the scrapping of existing plant and a massive investment in electronic engineering, but Vickers made no attempt at such a change. Rather the company's board of directors adapted to the new situation in a rather piecemeal fashion. They were to remain a mechanical engineering firm – that *was* Vickers. If arms contracts dried up they would survive in the commercial world as engineers. However such survival was more difficult than they realised – the 'service approach' had its limitations in the multinational market place.[2]

As an arms producer Vickers had provided the government with research and design facilities. However, with the second world war, and then in the 1950s the development of the nuclear bomb, the research and design of armaments became the direct concern of government. In this situation Vickers ran down the design teams at its major engineering plants. Scott, in his history of the company noted that: 'If [Vickers] produced comparatively little that was their own design this was no accident . . . The board had acted in the assumption that there would be a sufficiently large pool of existing designs to make a large engineering design staff unnecessary.'[3]

The assumption proved over-optimistic. The lack of imaginative new design greatly affected the competitive edge of the company's heavy engineering plants. An absence of investment in research and design was one thing, another (and more fatal) flaw was the absence of any overall financial discipline and control within the company. As a legacy of 'cost plus' detailed and centralised cost control was unheard of. Each of the major plants was left to its own devices. Within the company the central office was responsible only for external relations, the diplomacy of obtaining orders and raising finances. Without a central investment and product plan, local *ad hoc* decisions were made to take up excess capacity and the company was involved in an unconnected sprawl of products and production systems.[4]

During the 1960s these problems were becoming increasingly obvious. The company's aircraft interests were making gigantic losses and Vickers accepted the necessity of uniting with GEC, to form the British Aircraft Corporation. And aircraft production wasn't the only crisis point: profits in steel were low, the shipbuilding boom (which had subsidised parts of Vickers' operations) was over too. The general weakness of the engineering divisions could no longer be hidden. With all this, borrowings were high (£70 million in 1960 and still over £60 million in 1965), and competition was increasing in intensity.

A hell of a mess therefore; and by 1964 it had got through to the board of directors that something needed to be done. They decided to employ a team of management consultants to look over the operations. McKinsey – a top American firm – were called in and confirmed that the company was in a mess. A business journalist summed up the consultant's report in this way,

it encouraged greater consideration of the likely returns from an investment before money was spent, it suggested that Vickers should be organised on the basis of businesses which made profit instead of works which employed people, and it helped install a system of budgets and targets. Vickers it said, has been works oriented: it should now become market oriented.[5]

In *Vickers News*, the chairman, Sir Charles Dumphie, put the emphasis in a slightly different way: 'It is the basic purpose in all these schemes of modernisation and rationalisation that we should establish the conditions in which manpower – our most valuable asset – can operate at the highest level of productivity.'

Acting on the McKinsey report, Vickers and all of its wholly-owned subsidiaries were brought together as one company. From April 1965 Vickers became Vickers Ltd. This new company was organised into product-based divisions and the management of each division was responsible for its own profitability. But this 'shake up', while significant, was not particularly drastic. Certainly in 1965 Vickers Ltd. was not comparable with ITT. And it wasn't very profitable either: profits which had stood at a modest 5.8 per cent in 1956 fell to a disastrous 2.8 per cent in 1967. Dividends hadn't risen for over 10 years. It couldn't last . . . there was to come a time when the 'service attitude' – national institution or no – was to become too much of a financial liability.

Chapter 3

Shake Up!

Clearly Vickers Ltd. was due for a shake-up. When it came in 1970 it was a result of a well-orchestrated campaign organised by the company's institutional shareholders (whose holdings in Vickers at that time totalled £37.5 million/54.1 per cent of all shares). Of these the Prudential Insurance Company was the leading force, pressuring for a re-organisation of the company and an improvement in its profitability.

The main demand raised by the shareholders was for a tougher internal policy with more rigid financial controls, built around the office of managing director. The board responded and announced the changes in the 1970 Annual Report:

> We shall make some important changes in our top management structure. In a number of companies the offices of Chairman and Chief Executive have recently been separated. The changes we shall announce will be based on this principle, and the office of Chief Executive will carry with it wide executive powers and responsibility under the authority of the Board for the initiation and formulation of the commercial and financial policy of the company.

The City's view

The views of the shareholders were expounded in the pages of the financial press. Commentators on the 1970 Annual Report were all agreed on the need for a more ruthless and profit-orientated approach within the company. *The Times* put it like this: 'What is necessary is a careful pruning out of unprofitable or marginally profitable work. This would certainly involve the concentration of such varied engineering work in a smaller number of factories. And that inevitably means redundancies or the conversion of one or two large works to another more profitable activity.' The *Investors Chronicle* said the same thing: 'There are considerable areas in which Vickers can wield the company axe without detriment to turnover and with benefit to profits.' (14 May 1970) The *Financial Times* made it clear that management was culpable: 'What it has clearly not done in any material sense, is to rationalise out whole uneconomic units.' (18 May 1970)

For *The Times* the problem lay with: 'Sir Leslie's [the previous chairman] own feelings of humanity. He clearly jibs at any solution which will lead to premature retirement or redundancy for men who have worked for Vickers all their lives.' (6 May 1970) The *Daily Mail* saw this as a reflection of a more general malaise afflicting Vickers: 'Vickers Board have seemed more devoted to the national interest than to the shareholders. . . . the man wanted, the man for the job, the man tough enough to make Vickers the great armaments company fit for a peace-time world is Lord Beeching.'

The men for the job

The scene was set, therefore. Vickers' board of directors was forced to accept the necessity for change. In their search for new 'top men' who could carry out the task of restructuring the company they turned to the state sector. The *Daily Mail*'s choice was in great demand, but there was no shortage of senior industrialists who, as a consequence of their experience in the nationalised industries, knew how to take profitability seriously. Vickers appointed Peter Matthews from British Steel as managing director and later Lord Robens of the coal board joined Matthews as chairman. In 1971 the *Observer* noted that, 'Matthews is a quiet man, who gives an impression of calm, and even caution, but those who know him say that he is "ruthless as hell" and will not hesitate to prune middle management and make sure that the power lies in Millbank Tower.' (14 February 1971) After pointing to the areas of low profitability in the company, the article added, 'Matthews would certainly not retain these interests for sentimental reasons.'

Matthews' appointed task was to convert Vickers into an

effective, profit-conscious company, able to earn and increase its dividend. To do this he needed to establish centralised control over the company's finance. And that proved to be a big job. One commentator noted at the time that:

> Matthews is visibly shaken by the inadequacy of the figures that come into his office. Instead of the monthly profit and balance sheet figures that would be regarded as standard in any professionally run large company there is an inadequate system of annual forecasts and quarterly re-appraisements. In place of rigorously measuring deviations from plan and swiftly correcting them, there is a rather loose pattern of revising the forecasts. Inevitably, forecasts are not met, and when figures fell repeatedly below par last year they were received at head office with that air of blank surprise which infallibly marks a financially out-of-control organisation. Sorting out this appalling mess is Denis Groom's job, with a target of producing meaningful monthly accounts from April onwards. Then it is up to Matthews to make them stick and force the groups to regard meeting budgets as a serious priority. (*Sunday Times* 21 February 1971)

All this involved a reassessment of the organisation of production in the various plants, some of which had become almost autonomous units. The *Financial Times* pointed to the fact that two main engineering plants still had 'their own armaments division—a reminder of how each works was able to pursue its own diversification . . . Some of the older engineering divisions have acquired a momentum of their own that will take some stopping.' (19 February 1971)

This local autonomy and lack of a centralised financial control had produced a situation in Vickers where 70 per cent of the profits were coming from about 20 per cent of the assets. Something had to be done about the 80 per cent.

It was this scale of the problem which made a leading business commentator, writing in 1971, conclude that 'Lord Robens, and Peter Matthews have one of the most difficult tasks in British industry'. Driving the point home he said: 'Vickers must be a prime target for takeover by another company which would aim to sell off the assets it did not want'[1]. Many shareholders would have

The changing thoughts of
Lord Robens of Woldingham

Labour candidate for Wansbeck division of Northumberland

'The elementary right of the common people to have under common ownership the essential means of life was one that admitted of no compromise, and we might be sure that the powerful vested interests would fight bitterly to retain the wealth and privileges which common ownership would end.'
19 February 1945

'Is the country to be governed by the monopolists or by the people? Under a Labour government private enterprise would take second place.'
28 June 1945

Member of shadow cabinet

'I say to trade unionists as I am never tired of saying to employers that the surest way to high production is along the road of joint effort based on joint consultation. The economic situation of this country should be above politics and it was perhaps unfortunate that the country's position was thrown between two major political parties as being the fault of each other.'
1 January 1952

Shadow Minister of Labour

'The original object of strikes was to do some personal damage to the profitability of a company which also did damage to the private pocket of the owner. Times have changed. We have a managerial society in which the owners welcomed such a take-over, but as things have turned out they have received the benefits without all the financial disruption. As a consequence of their revolt the 'unprofitable assets' were chopped off or rationalised, the viability of the company improved, and the financial structure left undisturbed. They got the best of both worlds. In general the shareholders' reforming initiative was greeted with relief by management at Millbank Tower. As one of them put it: 'Looking back I would say that we were all pretty concerned about the way things were going, we had read the financial press and so on. I think most people welcomed Sir Peter's appointment. Certainly on hindsight – with the example of Rolls Royce – you could say that Vickers was heading the same way.'

So changes were made at the top. Matthews was determined to bring Vickers into the modern world of the giant corporations. This aim involved speeding up those tendencies established after the 1964 reorganisation, and carrying out the McKinsey recommendations without regard for sentiment and tradition. What had to be strongly affirmed was the fact that 'the business of business is *profit*'. Investment and marketing strategies had to be developed strictly in the pursuit of profitability and maximum returns.

In asserting the logic of profitability the new men were very successful. The basis of this success lay in the strict – and centralised – financial discipline which Matthews imposed. The 'Matthews system' has two aspects: first, no large expenditures can be made without central vetting. At the moment the limits are these: 1. a divisional manager can purchase spare parts, small tools, etc. but he cannot spend more than £3,000 on any item without the agreement of the works manager; 2. a works manager can buy larger items – a lorry or a safety guard – but nothing over £10,000 without the agreement of the group chairman; 3. the group chairman is able to make investment decisions on plant and machinery up to £30,000. By way of such limits Vickers' head office at Millbank Tower acts as the *central bank* for the corporation – and in the exercise of its banking function exerts real control over the way resources are developed in the plants. This control is aided by the second feature of the Matthews system: each division is required to make detailed monthly reports to Millbank Tower. In this way loss makers become quickly visible and, given the division of the company into the smallest possible viable units, responsibility for that loss is easily identifiable. Such a system gives the banker powerful control, and in 1977 Lord Robens made clear what this means at management level.

> Well, you have to take a hard line sometimes. And you know we can measure performance without much difficulty. It's not too hard with modern methods for us to have a fairly good hold of what is going on. If our bids for contracts are widely out, or if performance is not up to what it ought to be we have a change in management. As I said you have to take a hard line sometimes. Management is a profession and if someone is no good at it or, for some reason or another he isn't suited to it, he should get out.

This is the logic which has transformed Vickers and has placed the company on the fringe of the big league. The company still makes great play of the *decentralised* nature of its operations, the autonomy of local management and the beauty of smallness, but all this is established through rigorously enforced and centralised budgeting controls. So while a senior manager may observe that 'we don't charge in [to local plants or acquired companies] with big boots. The people at Millbank are there to assist the running of the business by providing information and advice', it is clear that there are big boots around and that a series of inadequate monthly reports will bring them out into the open. For this is the logic of the new era. It is centralised financial control – allied with stress upon the decentralised responsibility for profits – which provides the mechanism that determines the company's development. In its implementation the whole 'shape' of the company has altered.

'Disposals' and 'acquisitions'

In reporting these changes Vickers (like other companies) talks of 'disposal' and 'acquisitions'. Since 1968 Vickers has 'disposed' of a great variety of plant, factories, and sometimes entire operations. Usually a 'disposal' meant shut-down and redundancy. Printing machinery was badly hit as Vickers closed down its Crabtree works in London and at Water Lane in Leeds. On Tyneside the gradual yet inexorable run-down of heavy engineering at the Elswick and Scotswood works continued. Reorganisation of engineering production in the south ended with large numbers of redundancies at

VICKERS: Taking over, running down, selling off

Summary list of 'acquisitions' and 'disposals' of Vickers Ltd. 1965–1978 in Britain

'Acquisitions'

1965 Oxygenaire Ltd. (Basingstoke)
Vickers Roneo Ltd. (London and Liverpool)
Hans Zimmer (Frankfurt) and High
Polymer & Petro Chemicals Ltd. (London)
R.W. Crabtree & Sons Ltd.
(London, Gateshead and Leeds)

1966 Dawson, Payne & Lockett

1968 Algraphy Ltd.
Michell Bearings Ltd. (Newcastle)

1969 Hirst Buckley Ltd. (Sussex and Oldham)
Kirkby's Engineers Ltd. (Walsall)
Slingsby Sailplanes Ltd. (Kirkby Moorside)

1970 Brown Brothers Ltd. (Edinburgh)

1973 Dawson & Bates Manufacturing Ltd.
(Gomersal, Leeds and Thetford)

1974 Fanfold Ltd. (London); Middows Bros. Ltd.

1976 John Hastie Ltd. (Edinburgh);
Four Plus Ltd. (Oldham);
Kearney & Trecker Marwin Ltd. (Brighton)

1977 Joyce Leobe (Gateshead)

'Disposals'

1968 Metropolitan Cammell (Holdings) Ltd. (sold)
Part of Crayford (run down)
Vickers Naval Yard (sold)
Parts of Scotswood & Elswick (run down)
Factory at Bilston (sold)

1969 Olding Group (Hatfield & Scotland) (sold)

1970 International Computers (Holdings) Ltd. (sold)
Ioco Works (Glasgow) (closed)
Ship repair division at Palmers works (Tyneside) (closed)
Forge at Elswick (closed)

1971 Vickers All Wheel Drive (closed)
London Works of Crabtrees (closed)
All the Zimmer Companies (Chemical Engineering) (sold)
Robert Boby Works (Bury St Edmunds) (closed)
ABC Motors (Walton-on-Thames) (closed)
Kirkby's Engineers Ltd. (closed)

1975 Most of Water Lane Crabtree Works (closed)

1976 Barber-Greene England Ltd. (sold)

the South Marston works in Swindon. For the board these changes were 'particularly pleasing since they reflected the major effort that has been made in recent years to streamline the group and to discard those activities which could be indentified as lacking growth potential.'

As the 'old Vickers' was cut back a new firm was built through the take-over of new plants, operating in new areas of proven growth potential. Firms making office equipment, bottling machinery, glass fibre submarines were acquired as were a smaller number of traditional engineering manufacturers. The rapidity of these take-overs – and the consequent reshaping of Vickers – is quite startling. *By 1971 almost a third of the company's sales were from businesses acquired since 1964.* Even excluding the foreign take-overs the list of acquisitions is dramatic: in 1965 four companies were taken over, one in 1966, six in 1968, three in 1969, and one in 1970; another company was added to the list in 1973, followed by two in 1974 and a further three in 1976. This totals over twenty companies taken over in just eleven years.

One aspect of the underlying logic at work here is well illustrated by the case of Vickers Properties Ltd., a company which Vickers set up as a wholly-owned subsidiary during these years. While men like Jim Slater and John Bentley stole the headlines as 'asset strippers', companies like Vickers were also realising the advantage of manipulating 'property' to their advantage: during the years of the property boom most of the giant corporations set up subsidiary property companies.

The closures and run-downs also 'disposed' of the workers, who left behind them empty shops and unused land: resources which (in the crazy logic of the market place) gained in value. In 1972 the Vickers' board (after a careful study of 'property values' and discussions with leading figures in the property investment business), transferred large pieces of land and empty plant to Vickers Property Ltd. On Tyneside seven acres of the Scotswood Road works (which covered four of the old engineering shops) were transferred, as was a three acre site at Romford. The old Hoe Crabtree works in Southwark which had been closed in 1971 and a large part of the South Marston site were also transferred. This trend has continued over the past six years (most of the valuable inner-city site of the Water Lane works in Leeds as well as more of the empty Elswick and Scotswood shops on Tyneside being affected) and by 1976 the capital employed by Vickers Properties was £38 million, 24 per cent of Vickers' total capital. Comparing Vickers' property interests with its factories and industrial plant we see that the value of its 'properties' amount to over a third of the value of its 'productive assets'. The irony of the engineering giant turned estate agent is interesting in itself. What it also serves to make clear is the extent to which the 'new Vickers' had been transformed by the logic of profit. The average yield from property, especially (in the early 1970s) office property, and later from warehousing, tended to be greater than the average yield from mechanical engineering. Hence the switch, and the change in the contours of the Tyne as warehouses replaced engineering shops.

Vickers' global reach

These changes in the nature of Vickers' operations in Britain are also reflected in the development of its overseas interests. Historically, Vickers has been closely tied to Britain and (apart from an early colonial venture in Canada) did not set up factories abroad. After the war the need for new markets and higher rates of return led Vickers to think about producing overseas. Since the Commonwealth offered all the advantages of 'friendly' governments, no tariffs and a plentiful supply of land and labour, Vickers acquired heavy engineering companies in Australia and followed this by reacquiring its naval and engineering interests in Canada. In 1959 the company briefly extended its Commonwealth base by joining with Babcock & Wilcox to establish a heavy engineering company in West Bengal.

But this was still a very minor part of their operations. Today, however, the situation is transformed. In the early 1960s there were virtually no Vickers' subsidiaries in Europe. By 1976 there were eleven in France, four in Holland, three in Sweden, two in Spain, one in Germany, and one in Norway. Since 1956 and the formation of the Common Market, Europe – rather than any particular national state – has increasingly served as a unified market and production unit for the giant corporations. Vickers – rather belatedly – followed this pattern. European take-overs formed a basic part of its strategy to regroup away from its 'traditional'

The changing world of Vickers

sectors. Firms producing office equipment and lithographic plates were acquired in Europe and linked up with Roneo and Howson Algraphy in Britain. This process of internationalisation also extended to South Africa: a country which offered profit-conscious corporations the infrastructure and the consumer market of an industrialised country along with the low wage rates of a colony. Vickers had only one subsidiary there in the early 1960s; by 1976 it had seven, and its rate of investment there shows no signs of slowing down.[2]

Such are the changes brought about under 'the Matthews system'. They have drastically altered Vickers, and they represent just one – particularly stark – expression of the transformation that is generally taking place within British companies based in 'traditional' industrial sectors. In the face of the growing international competition offered by the large multinational corporations, companies like Vickers have been forced to change. While the company is still only a fringe member of the corporate economy its ambitions are clearly set in that direction. But Vickers hasn't done all this on its own – it received considerable assistance and support from the government and the tax payer. No account of the making of the 'new Vickers' would be complete without an examination of this.

Chapter 4

The Helping Hand of the State

Vickers has always had a close relationship with the government. In the past, as we have seen, this relationship was governed by the needs of national defence. But even then it went beyond government arms orders and a guaranteed profit margin. In peace time armament manufacturing capacity still had to be maintained to ensure rapid rearmament in the event of war. So, in the 'national interest', governments always subsidised Vickers and directed civilian orders towards it during periods of slack.

Paradoxically, the new Vickers – a minor armaments producer – has continued to benefit from state support. We saw earlier how the ailing aircraft factories within Vickers were rescued by a state-organised merger with GEC. Vickers accepted this assistance gladly. The company was making huge losses and it was becoming clear that the post-war aircraft industry was not to be a place for medium-sized firms. The creation of BAC was not an isolated incident. It set the pattern for a general change in the role of the state in Britain which demonstrated, in clear terms, the truth that Bevan saw in 1944.

In the post-war period the modern capitalist economy has been dependent upon the active role of the state in industry. This development has called for many adjustments in established political thinking. Perhaps the most dramatic (more an about-turn than an adjustment) was associated with the Tory government under Edward Heath. Elected on a programme aimed at releasing the 'invigorating' forces of 'free enterprise', the reality of Rolls Royce and Upper Clyde Shipbuilders convinced the Tory government that the conditions for 'laissez-faire' capitalism no longer existed in Britain. Given the growing international corporate economy, weaker companies needed to be supported, and the

This is one thing we've never had to do.

We have never had to ask the British taxpayer to prop us up.

"Never" for Vickers means the last 150 years, including over 100 as a public company.

Through all those years, for generation after generation, we have earned profits, paid taxes, re-invested, provided employment and lived up to our motto—"Service in peace and war".

We have great traditions, but the greatest of them all is the ability to stand on our own feet.

Some of the activities for which we are famous are now scheduled to pass into other hands. If they do, we hope they will retain enough of Vickers' traditions to keep them alive, well and in profit.

In all our other activities, a great array of products and services, in Britain and across the world, we shall continue to do what we have always done—adapt, pioneer, make and sell without expecting the taxpayer to prop us up.

"We", let it be added, are not only the tens of thousands who work in Vickers, but also the multitude of small investors who have a stake in Vickers—38,000 directly and scores of thousands more through pension funds and other forms of institutional investment.

powerful ones (from Britain and abroad) needed to be attracted by grants, loans and other assistance. The acceptable face of capitalism turned out to be the state. In 1972 the Heath government's Industry Act provided £1 billion to help companies invest. This was taken up and expanded by Labour governments during the 'crisis years' that followed. Vickers, like the rest, benefited from this.

Vickers has needed a lot of help from the government.[1] The new investment programme for the South Marston site in Swindon was established with the aid of a £6 million grant. In Leeds the Howson Algraphy plant received £2 million and the new plant established for Michel Bearings on Tyneside was built with the aid of £450,000 from the British government and £2.5 million pounds from the EEC. Government aid has been plentiful and without too many strings attached. It has simply helped the Vickers board to achieve the targets that it has set itself. On no occasion has the government intervened to direct investment in particular directions or toward particular areas of need. This absence was made clear at the time of the Water Lane closure. In spite of a special grant fund to aid investment in the printing machinery industry the plant in Leeds was allowed to close. The company requested no assistance and none was offered.[2]

But the handouts have not been restricted to cash payments; recently the company has received a great deal of help from the government in its acquisition of two firms – Hastie Brothers on Clydeside and the Brighton machine tool manufacturer Kearney and Trecker Marwin (KTM). The government arranged these deals and provided the further assistance of a £2.5 million loan to Hasties and £10 million (in debts written off, loans and payments) at KTM. Not bad you might think! It's clear that the Vickers' Board was quite pleased too. The take-over of KTM (something which senior management insist 'we never looked for') was celebrated by a party at Millbank Tower with representatives from the Department of Industry as guests of honour! It's worth looking at both cases in detail.

Handouts at Brighton and on the Clyde

First, KTM. The company which is now KTM came under the control of the American group Kearney and Trecker, one of the world's most famous machine tool makers, in 1966. A first injection of state funds came in 1970 when the Industrial Re-organisation Corporation (a product of the Wilson administration) and the Midland Bank Finance Corporation each bought £300,000 of non-voting shares. Then Walter Norton, the machine tool merchant described as an 'ebulliant entrepreneur', came on the scene (it was Norton who was later to appeal to the High Court, questioning the way in which Vickers got control of KTM.) In June 1972 he bought a 50 per cent share in the company for £5 million. In 1973 the Department of Industry assisted in a merger between Kearney Trecker and the machine tool division of Marwin. The outcome of the merger was a company with the broadest range of numerical controlled machine tools in Europe – a European com-petitor of the US giant Cincinnati Milacron.

The new company, however, was based upon a very shaky financial structure, and under the combined effects of the three day week and one of the worst recessions in machine tools since the 1930s, faced a serious financial crisis. Because of its leading position in a sector regarded by the government as central to the re-generation of British industry, the Department of Industry swiftly moved in to buy a 50 per cent share and provide £3.5 million pounds worth of capital. This intervention was a simple propping-up operation. The Labour government had no intention of nationalising the machine tool industry, or of linking KTM with Alfred Herbert, the Coventry-based machine tool company which was already under state control. In fact the government was embarrassed by any such suggestion and made it clear that they were providing financial assistance to KTM but wanted no control of the company. To demonstrate this they gave the job of managing and restructuring the finances of the company to Vickers. In return Vickers had the promise of an option on taking a majority share-holding in April 1976.

In the following two years KTM made what was described as a 'dramatic' recovery from a trading loss of £1.42 million to profits of £46,000. Vickers – as the company in the driver's seat – was in a strong position to press its option of purchase – and on extremely favourable terms.[3] The government wrote off £5.2 million of liabilities, gave £1.9 million of financial assistance together with an unsecured loan of £1 million, and bought £900,000 in new non-voting shares. Vickers' contribution (£803,000 for 86 per cent of the voting equity, together with a loan of £500,000 and a guarantee of £250,000 of the government's loan) pales in comparison.

Walter Norton complained, there was a parliamentary debate, Dennis Skinner walked through the 'no' lobby, and the KTM shop stewards in Brighton protested about the absence of any real planning in the industry: 'At the moment we're competing against each other. It's ridiculous, its anarchy.' But it *was* a good deal – for Vickers. And it was soon to be followed by another one.

Hastie Brothers of Greenock had been a highly successful family firm. It was a leading European producer of steering gears for ships and had started to develop a particularly advanced type of high pressure pump. But the company was undercapitalised and held to be badly managed. In 1975 the two major shareholders, Lithgow (Holdings) Ltd. and the Weir Group Ltd. came to an arrangement with the Department of Industry to support the parent company with new capital of over £1 million provided between the three of them. (At that time the government had sought the advice of Vickers through its wholly-owned subsidiary Brown Brothers – Hasties' main British competitor – who offered the opinion that it would take £5 million to put Hasties in order.) But losses continued and at the end of October the shareholders called in the receiver.

Throughout this period the workforce at Hasties were concerned about the future of their jobs. The stewards committee had met Gerald Kaufman, the Under Secretary at the Department of Industry. One of the stewards reported on his response to their central question:

We asked him 'If at the end of the day, a buyer cannot be found for Hasties, will the government take it over?' And he replied, 'I'm not prepared to answer, but I certainly don't want that. I certainly don't want to nationalise it.'

The stewards received more straight answers from the receiver:

We were pretty shattered, but he said to us, 'Don't get too despondent, I'm not here as liquidator, in fact you're ahead of the game here.' He was referring to the fact that Brown Bros. had already been in and had had a look around. They seemed favourably impressed and had stated their interest in taking over Hasties. On this basis he thought he'd only be in Hasties for about two weeks.

He was, in most essentials, right. By the end of December, Hasties was part of Vickers' Oceanics Division; moreover the government had withdrawn all its voting rights but increased its financial assistance.

Another good deal for Vickers. Hasties' workers aren't so sure about it though. Vickers wasn't prepared to take over without a 'slimming down' of the workforce, and two hundred men were consigned to the lengthy dole queues on the Clyde. But that's part of another story which we shall be returning to.

Nationalisation: from steel to shipyards

The state handouts are only one side of the coin which has produced the new Vickers corporation. While the state has been giving aid – in the form of grants, loans, and preferred options – it has also been *taking over* large parts of the old Vickers. Steel, shipyards and aircraft production have all been brought directly under the states' umbrella and the company compensated accordingly.

Big business has always welcomed state handouts, and since the war there has been a dramatic shift in its attitude to state take-overs. There were signs of the changes to come in the way the coal owners approached nationalisation. An undercapitalised coal industry, wrecked by the most blatant of profiteering, was auctioned off to the state, and the miners and the rest of us are still paying off the price of that 'compensation'. The logic behind successive Labour governments' approaches to nationalisation has been consistent. It was clearly stated by Lord Robens when in 1960 as shadow Minister of Labour he argued for the re-nationalisation of the steel industry on the grounds that the industry was not efficient and that state ownership was 'vital to the economic planning of the nation's affairs'. As Chairman of Vickers Ltd. he still holds to these views. And the chairmen of other companies have come to recognise that nationalisation has a role to play in modern capitalist economy.

The history of Vickers since the war highlights this pattern of change within the business community. During the post-war

Labour governments Vickers fought strongly against the nationalisation of steel and attempted to 'hive off' some 80 per cent of its steel plants (particularly those in Sheffield) on the grounds that they fell outside the steel industry. By the late 1960s – and after a Tory denationalisation – the situation looked quite different. While 'hiving off' was still a common practice, companies like Vickers were glad to be rid of undercapitalised, burdensome plant. Glad too for the compensation. In Vickers' case this totalled some £16 million, cash which permitted the take-overs of Crabtrees, Roneo, Howson Algraphy and Michell Bearings, and laid the foundations of a profitable commercial engineering group. The compensated nationalisation of Vickers shipyards and aircraft interests (negotiated between 1977 and 1978) followed a similar pattern.

In the formation of British Aircraft Corporation Vickers and GEC had already recognised that in a highly capitalised and competitive international aerospace industry there was room for just one British producer. They recognised too that state support (through contracts, research and development, direct aid and allowances) was essential. The nationalisation of BAC became a logical extension of this process. So much was this the case that BAC and the other aerospace companies co-operated with Lord Beswick (chairman designate of British Aerospace) and the Aerospace Organising Committee long before the industry was legally nationalised. The *Financial Times* was quite clear about the reasons for this and the need for nationalisation. An election with a Tory victory would kill the bill but 'that would . . . still leave the industry's problems – especially the shortage of civil work – untouched and by then in even more need of a solution'. It went on to point to

the growing concern in the industry over the long term future, and the uncaring recognition that while, politically, nationalisation is unpalatable to many people, it is likely to be the only way the government will be induced to subscribe the large sums . . . needed.

Without nationalisation, in the harsher commercial conditions of the 1980s and with the increased costs and greater technological complexity of civil and military aircraft, no single UK company would be able to compete alone in world markets, and a combination of the industry's resources would be a fundamental condition of even getting into the markets, let alone succeeding in them.

Even with nationalisation and state support, Lord Beswick senses that 'there are hazards ahead'. Hazards mainly represented by the industry's over-capacity. 'I have steadfastly refused to give any guarantee that every job at every site can be secured with current orders . . . A record of genuine profitability is the best agreement for any programme for more investment.' (*Financial Times* 8 March 1977)

Neither Vickers nor GEC challenged the logic of nationalisation. If there was to be a struggle it was to be over the terms. And Vickers – to quote their chairman – intended putting up 'one helluva fight' to get the maximum possible compensation money.

The shipyards were a little different and their case warrants close inspection. Vickers once had shipyards on the Tyne but as a result of the Geddes Report these were amalgamated with Swan Hunters. Vickers had a 25 per cent shareholding which it sold in the late 1960s. By 1976 Vickers' shipyard interests were concentrated in Barrow in Furness – the company town on the west coast which then still represented a powerful centre of the Vickers Corporation. Barrow was virtually owned by Vickers. The company's presence is found in the names of streets and pubs. The local fourth division football team appeared in the list of Vickers' assets. Barrow lay at the heart of the old Vickers.

And it was profitable too. In the last two years under Vickers' ownership the ship building division provided around a fifth of the total profits for the company. Vickers' yards were mainly naval yards,[4] protected from the crisis which was hitting commercial shipping. The Vickers' yards had a virtual monopoly of naval submarines; they were also the best yards for large battleships like the through deck cruiser. And – as in the old days – the pricing and costing on these regular naval orders always ensured a comfortable profit margin. In their desire to keep these yards the naval producers set up a 'naval consortium' – a device to separate themselves off from the commercial shipping interests. This move by Vickers, Vospers and Cammell Laird was open and quite blatant. At other times it might have worked. At that particular time – and in the context of Barrow – it was unlikely to do so.

In the early years of the 1974 Labour government 'national-isation' appeared again as a central political issue. The 'social contract' with the trade unions was contingent upon certain of the 'higher reaches of power' being captured through state ownership. To accede to a nationalised shipbuilding industry which included only the ropiest of the assets (while continuing to buy warships at preferred prices from private yards) was simply not politically viable. This national pressure was compounded by the situation in Barrow itself.

'Nationalisation' meant a lot in Barrow and the support for it was especially strong within the unions and Labour Party in the town. Eric Montgomery, convenor in the yards for eight years and AUEW district secretary for seven, described how

> there's always been pressure for nationalisation; it's been
> increasingly recently. It's been expressed through every
> channel, the individual unions, the Confed and the Labour
> Party. This has always been met by a campaign against
> nationalisation orchestrated by the *Barrow News*.

This support for nationalisation (far stronger than on, say, Tyneside or Merseyside) reflected the accumulated unease that working people in the town felt toward the power Vickers had wielded over generations of their families – over their working lives and the education and the future of their children (all further education in the town was geared to the requirements of the yards). An unease in which feelings of hostility toward the power of the company meshed with the relative security of employment that had been associated with work in the yards.

In the 1920s a director of Vickers had said that 'grass would grow in the yards if the people at Barrow elected a Labour MP'. These words are remembered – as are the more recent activities of the company. A local party official puts it like this:

> Vickers have had virtually complete control over the influx of
> industry into the area. Industries which they have not wanted
> they have always been able to turn away. When there was a
> Tory council they did it directly through the council. When there

was a Labour council Vickers exerted pressure by trying to buy the land set aside for the new company, by preventing them from having access to various essential facilities, by making statements through the paper about the harm the new industry will bring to Barrow and by influencing local government officers. You can never pin it down, but one example is that there was talk of the car industry coming to Barrow. Everybody would have been very much in favour of this, except Vickers. And so it did not come.

Given this monopoly power exercised by private capital, nationalisation seemed to make a lot of sense. The naval consortium was beaten off and the yards nationalised. Again, Vickers shareholders were compensated; but in the town little has changed.

Eric Montgomery's own experience tells the story. When he failed to be re-elected as AUEW district secretary Vickers would not let him have his job back, in spite of an unwritten, but always hitherto practised, agreement that workers in Barrow who become union officers would always have a job in the yards when their term of office was finished. When nationalisation came in, Montgomery thought things might change:

> My case was raised again with management. But the same people who said before that under no circumstances, now or in the future, would they take me back are the ones who are in charge now. And they've said it again, and have every intention to go on saying it. When the case was taken to Kaufman and Varley, they said that the local management – Vickers' management – have complete authority; but then when you go to this management on wages they say they've got no authority.

So what does that make him feel in general about nationalisation?

> Well, put it this way, over the negotiating tables, one of those most violently opposed to nationalisation was Richardson, the chairman of Vickers Shipbuilding Group, and there was I, one of the strongest advocates of nationalisation. Now, after nationalisation, he's on the nationalised board and I'm on the streets. That's nationalisation 1977 style.

In this respect – the retention of the old managerial personnel –

The Modern Vickers

A.B.C. Motors Ltd.
ACC-Vickers-Babcock Ltd. *India*
C. Baker Instruments Ltd.
Mathias Bauerle GmbH. *Germany*
Robert Boby Ltd.
Bratby & Hinchcliffe Ltd.
British Acheson Electrodes Ltd.
Brown Brothers & Co. Ltd.
   John Greig & Sons Ltd.
Campbells & Hunter Ltd.
Canadian Vickers Ltd. *Canada*
   Montreal Ship Repairs Ltd. *Canada*
Compact Orbital Gears Ltd.
Cooke, Troughton & Simms Ltd.
Crabtree Foundry Co. Ltd.
Crabtree-Mann Ltd.
Crabtree-Vickers (Canada) Ltd. *Canada*
Crabtree-Vickers Inc. *U.S.A.*
   Howson-Algraphy, Inc. *U.S.A.*
Crabtree-Vickers Ltd.
Crabtree-Vickers-Pension-Trust Ltd.
Dawson-Aquamatic Ltd.
Dawson & Barfos Manufacturing Ltd.
Dawson Bros. Ltd.
Dawson, Payne & Elliott Ltd.
Elless Feeder Co. of Europe Ltd.
Fillite (Runcorn) Ltd.
Four Plus Ltd.
Generale Resine Sud S.p.A., Cia. *Italy*
Graham-Enoch Manufacturing Co. Ltd.
John Hastie of Greenock (Holdings) Ltd.
   John Hastie of Greenock Ltd.
Howson-Algraphy Ltd.
   Howson-Algraphy AB *Sweden*
   Howson-Algraphy, B.V. *Holland*
   Howson-Algraphy (Europe) B.V. *Holland*
   Howson Algraphy (France) S.A. *France*
   Howson-Algraphy S.A. *Spain*
   Howson Algraphy S.A.R.L. *Lebanon*
   Howson Algraphy S.p.A. *Italy*
Howson Langham Equipment Ltd.
W. H. Howson Ltd.
Industrial and Commercial Research Ltd.
International Research & Development Co.
   Ltd.

J.O.C. Engineers Ltd.
Joyce-Loebl Ltd.
Kearney & Trecker Marwin Ltd.
Friedrich Kocks (U.K.) Ltd.
The Lyon Street Railway Co. Ltd.
Malting Technology International Ltd.
Malting Technology International Ltd. *Eire*
Metchair Ltd.
Michell Bearings Ltd.
Microscopes Nachet S.A. *France*
Millbank Development Services Ltd.
Otley Printing and Allied Machinery Ltd.
Oxygenaire Ltd.
Oyster Lane Properties (Holdings) Ltd.
   Oyster Lane Properties Ltd.
Patra Vickers Ltd. *Indonesia*
Robert Powley & Sons Ltd.
RV Hydratools Ltd.
Racine Hydraulik A/S *Denmark*
Roevac Automation Ltd.
Rolls-Royce and Associates Ltd.
Roneo Vickers Ltd.
   Art Metal Construction Co. Ltd.
   Antonio Corono S.p.A. *Italy*
   Ertma S.A. *Switzerland*
   Esco Ltd.
   Fanfold Ltd.
      Fanforms Ltd.
      Mani-Fold Forms Ltd.
   Hadewe B.V. *Holland*
   Langdon Precision Engineers Ltd.
   Roneo-Neopost Ltd.
   Roneo S.A., Cie du *France*
      Behin-Robustacier-Meubles S.A.
         France
      Columbia S.A. *France*
      Européenne de Réalisation *France*
      d'Organisation et de Participation, Sté.
      Immobilière de la Sente Giraud, Sté.
         France
      SPES, Sté. *France*
   Roneo Vickers Belgium S.A. *Belgium*
   Roneo Vickers Business Forms Ltd.
      Data-Flow Ltd.
      Datacopy Ltd.

Roneo Vickers Canada Ltd. *Canada*
Roneo Vickers Holland N.V. *Holland*
  Amato N.V.
  Assmann Kantoormachines N.V.
   Holland
  Daro Kantoormachines N.V. *Holland*
  Roneo Kantoormachines N.V. *Holland*
  Victor Kantoormachines N.V. *Holland*
Roneo Vickers Inc. *U.S.A.*
Roneo Vickers India Ltd. *India*
Roneo Vickers Norge A/S *Norway*
Roneo Vickers Overseas Ltd.
Roneo Vickers Partitions Ltd.
Roneo Vickers Svenska AB *Sweden*
  Berg Bolinder AB *Sweden*
Seaclean International Ltd.
Silica Fillers Ltd.
Slingsby Sailplanes Ltd.
The Supermarine Aviation Works (Vickers)
  Ltd.
Vickers (Agricultural) Ltd.
Vickers America Inc. *U.S.A.*
  Vickers American Medical Corp. *U.S.A.*
   Vickers Medical Products Corp. *U.S.A.*
Vickers-Armstrongs (Engineers) Ltd.
Vickers-Armstrongs Ltd.
Vickers-Armstrongs (Shipbuilders) Ltd.
Vickers-Armstrongs (Tractors) Ltd.
Vickers and Bookers Ltd.
Vickers (Finance) Ltd.
  Astbury & Madeley Holdings Ltd.
  Commonwealth Development Finance Co.
   Ltd.
  Tyne Tanker Cleaning Co. Ltd.
Vickers (Great Britain Holdings) GmbH.
  Germany
  Vickers (Great Britain) GmbH. *Germany*
Vickers Holdings Pty. Ltd. *Australia*
  Australian Innovation Corp. Ltd. *Australia*
  Middows Bros. Pty. Ltd. *Australia*
  Roneo Duplicators Pty. Ltd. *Australia*
   Industrial & Office Equipment Pty. Ltd.
    Australia
   Roneo Systems Pty. Ltd. *Australia*
   Roneo Vickers (Queensland) Pty. Ltd.
    Australia
   Roneo Vickers (South Australia) Pty.
    Ltd. *Australia*
   Roneo Vickers (Victoria) Pty. Ltd.
    Australia
  Vickers-Armstrongs (Australia) Pty. Ltd.
   Australia
  Vickers Australia Ltd. *Australia*
   Industrial Sales Ltd. *Australia*
   Uniteers Vickers Pte. Ltd. *Australia*
   Vickers Engineers (W.A.) Pty. Ltd.
    Australia
    Vickers Keogh Pty. Ltd. *Australia*

  W.A. Mining Engineering Services
   Pty. Ltd *Australia*
  Vickers Founders Pty. Ltd *Australia*
  Vickers Steelworks Pty. Ltd. *Australia*
   Aimto Pty. Ltd. *Australia*
   Vickers Adams Pty. Ltd. *Australia*
   Vickers Patra P.T. *Indonesia*
   Vickers Research Pty. Ltd. *Australia*
  Vickers Cockatoo Dockyard Pty. Ltd.
   Australia
  Vickers Graphics Pty. Ltd. *Australia*
  Vickers Sales Pty. Ltd. *Australia*
Vickers Instruments Inc. *U.S.A.*
Vickers Instruments Ltd.
Vickers (Insurance) Ltd.
Vickers-Intertek Ltd.
Vickers-McKay Ltd.
Vickers New Zealand Ltd. *New Zealand*
Vickers (Nominees) Ltd.
Vickers Oceanics Ltd.
  Fred Olsen Oceanics A/S *Norway*
Vickers Offshore (Projects and
  Developments) Ltd.
  Aylmer Engineering Co. Ltd.
  Vickers Subsea Ltd.
Vickers Oil Spill Clearance Ltd.
  Vikoma International Ltd.
Vickers Overseas Supplies Ltd.
Vickers (Pakistan) Ltd. *Pakistan*
Vickers Printing Machinery Group (Service)
  Ltd.
Vickers Properties Ltd.
  Inter-Vickers Ltd.
  Swindon Trading Estates Ltd.
Vickers (Securities) Ltd.
Vickers Seerdrum Ltd.
Vickers (Services) Ltd.
Vickers Southern Africa (Pty.) Ltd. *South
  Africa*
  Cooke, Troughton & Simms (Pty.) Ltd.
   South Africa
  Howson-Algraphy South Africa (Pty.) Ltd.
   South Africa
  Oxygenaire (South Africa) (Pty.) Ltd.
   South Africa
  Pinalex Investments (Pty.) Ltd. *South
   Africa*
  Roneo Manufacturing (Pty.) Ltd. *South
   Africa*
  Roneo Vickers South Africa (Pty.) Ltd.
   South Africa
  Vickers (Engineering) (Pty.) Ltd. *South
   Africa*
  Vickers Instruments (Pty.) Ltd. *South
   Africa*
Waite & Saville Ltd.
R. W. Webster & Co. Ltd.
G. J. Worrsam & Son Ltd.

nationalisation 1977 style is not much different from 1974 or 1964 style. Steelworkers, railwayworkers, and most of all the miners, have experienced the bitterness of working for the same boss as ownership changed hands. And something else has remained the same too. The 'naval consortium' was to an important degree the exception that proves a rule. For while Vickers was losing the public battle over the future of the naval yards it was involved in a detailed and discreet process of hiving-off one of its most promising shipbuilding assets. These assets – associated with the development of the North Sea oil field – never became a part of British Shipbuilders.

The development of the North Sea oilfield – particularly as it spreads beyond the continental shelf – is dependent upon the use of sophisticated underwater operations and installations. Vickers – through its submarine production – was well established in this field and the company was determined to retain these operations and reap the profits of the 1970s oil rush. In 1972 Vickers had set up a company called 'Oceanics'. This was created jointly with the National Research Development Corporation (26.31 per cent) and James Fisher & Sons – Shipowners (10.53 per cent) to specialise in underwater services of various sorts: work for the navy in recovering torpedoes, work for the GPO in laying cables, work for universities in getting samples from the sea bed etc. 'Oceanics' was a small and separate operation. At this time companies like Brown Bros. (the Edinburgh-based marine engineering firm, acquired by Vickers) and Slingsby Sailplanes (acquired in 1969 in order to apply techniques of glass fibre and plastic production to Vickers' submarines production) were – and logically so – part of the shipbuilding group. This fact was recognised by the company in 1973 when its *Annual Report* noted the growth potential of Vickers' underwater operations within the shipbuilding group. By 1974, however, things had changed. To quote from the *Annual Report*: 'Three businesses previously included in the shipbuilding group for reasons of administrative convenience though not engaged in shipbuilding, have now been brought together under the general heading of "Offshore Engineering".'

Glass fibre submarines, it seems, were no longer part of shipbuilding in the way that metal submarines were. Whatever the reasons – and readers can make their own judgements – the administrative shift had (for the company) the happy coincidence of placing what had been described as 'the jewel in Vickers crown' outside the orbit of nationalisation. Another good deal. And this wasn't the end of the story.

In 1975 Vickers Offshore Division centred upon an office with about fifteen technical and managerial staff. By May 1976 the staffing had increased to fifty and the following June – on the vesting day for British Shipbuilding – VOD employed 120 managers, project engineers and technicians. Almost all of this growth was achieved by internal transfers from the shipbuilding group. Again, whatever the reasons, the fact remained that Vickers retained within its Offshore Division a large proportion of the technical and scientific expertise that had accumulated in its shipbuilding operations. By the same token Vickers' gain was British Shipbuilders' loss. The potentially profitable growth centre of North Sea Oil – 'our oil' as it has been called – was to be the domain of private capital.

Part 2

THE HIDDEN COSTS OF VICKERS' GROWTH

On most economic indicators – share quotations, capital structure, growth and profit etc. – Vickers Ltd. in 1978 is a far healthier prospect than it was ten years ago. The company appeared in the *Observer* newspaper's new year honours list of good prospects for investors. Articles in the financial press no longer ridicule the 'service element' in the company but seriously discuss Vickers' prospects after nationalisation and the latest dose of government compensation. It is clear that today Vickers, while not a really big fish, is certainly seen as a professional outfit, fit to swim in the same pond as the rest. In many ways it's a bit of a success story – a modest one perhaps, but certainly no failure.

But to look at the Vickers' story in this way is to ignore entirely the way in which the people who work on the many shop floors and in the offices of the company and who live in communities which depend on it, have been affected by these changes. To ignore this, and to equate corporate 'modernness' and 'business success' with something called human progress, is to paint a partial picture, even a completely false one. We need to look much more closely at the Vickers' story.

To begin with it's perhaps important to point out that the workers – the numbers in the accounting system – were seriously affected by the changes we have described although they certainly weren't their instigators. In fact they were hardly involved in the relevant decisions at all. Good or bad they were on the receiving end. In the centralised modern corporation the important decisions are made at the top and those most affected by them are almost always the last to know.

At first sight this might all seem to be a question of 'information'. Certainly shop stewards at Vickers complain frequently about the

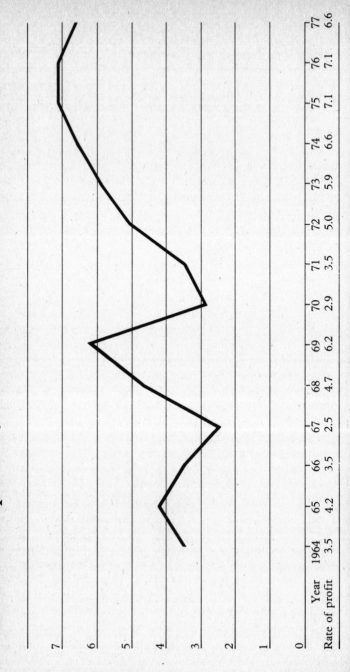

Vickers' rate of profit net profits, net assets

Year	1964	65	66	67	68	69	70	71	72	73	74	75	76	77
Rate of profit	3.5	4.2	3.5	2.5	4.7	6.2	2.9	3.5	5.0	5.9	6.6	7.1	7.1	6.6

lack of it; about not knowing what the hell is happening until it comes through along the office 'grapevine'. An ironic example of this took place at Michell Bearing Plant on Tyneside – Vickers' showpiece in the north east. Here the workers were informed that they were to be moved from the old factory into a new plant that was to be built alongside. A new plant, remember, that was built out of 'public' funds. Although it was to be their place of work, they were in no way involved in the decisions over the design and layout of the plant. It turned out that the showpiece had been built without windows. The men refused to work 'like battery hens'. Walls had to be partly dismantled and rearranged. Meanwhile the men park their cars in what is but a corner of a massive new car park. They assume that this expanse of tarmac is in some way related to the construction work that is going on around them on the new site. They assume that a new plant will be opened sometime – but they've not been told so. They know nothing of the company's plans for the site – the kinds of product to be produced, the nature and size of the labour force – *nothing*. As one man put it: 'We cannot get any information out of them. That's the situation with Vickers; it's always the same.'

This complaint is a general one. Vickers, say some, is like the Vatican. Everything is done behind closed doors. No doubt the extent to which the company keeps things tight would be criticised on courses in the leading business schools. Vickers – in business parlance – could be seen to have a 'communication problem'. The value of 'involvement' and day to day 'participation' is, after all, stressed increasingly in the business community. When Wills, the Bristol tobacco company, moved its workforce across to a new factory in Hartcliffe, teams of interviewers and industrial psychologists were involved in ascertaining the workers' feelings of lighting, wall colours, toilet facilities and the rest. 'Involvement' is good business practice, and there are signs that Vickers – in this sense too – is moving with the times. Workers, in some plants are consulted when management are deciding on the purchase of a new machine: 'There've been so many cock-ups in the past and with the money these new machines cost they think they'd better try to get it right'. And generally the company is adopting a more sophisticated approach to the value of its labour as a 'resource'. But what Vickers insist on – as do all the 'new' industrial psychologies – is that 'labour', for all its complexity, has to keep its place. Consultation may be in order, but only if it fits into a managerial hierarchy in which power remains concentrated at the top.

The truth of this was made clear by Lord Robens in the 1974 *Annual Report*. 'Consultation' he argued should take place between those carrying the responsibility for 'planning and direction' and those who are contributing 'other skills and functions'. The power of the planner and the path along which he directs the company is taken for granted. So too are the consequences that such planning can have for the people affected by it. For in this view the men and women who work on factory floors work there because their skills and abilities are fitted to that purpose. Such people have a common interest with those whose (supposedly higher) abilities fit them to plan and direct. As a consequence discussions between workers and management, to quote Robens once again, 'will be fruitful only to the degree that those taking part recognise a common interest and generally seek to reach conclusions serving that interest'.

But this assumption of a common interest is not one that can be made lightly. While few of the people who work on the factory floor regret the passing of the 'old Vickers' (its inefficiencies were all too clear) they have mixed feelings about the way things have changed. Many of them question the kinds of 'efficiency' that is being enforced within Vickers and the world of the giant corporations generally. In examining the changing nature of this (or any other) company, therefore, it is important that we go beyond the accounting scheme of 'profit and loss' and enquire into the broader, *social* costs and benefits of such changes. There have, in part one, already been hints of such social costs (plant closures, redundancies etc.). Part two examines these in detail. It looks at the ways in which Vickers' workers, their families and the localities in which they live, have been affected by the rationalisation that has taken place within the company.

Chapter 5

Taken Over

The 'new Vickers' was created through take-overs – a business practice which clearly reveals where the power lies in industry. No ballots are taken on the shop floor asking 'would you like to change your employer?' Nor is the sale of shares normally a matter to be discussed on consultation committees. The workers (and some of the managers) in the old Vickers' plants have lost count of the number of companies Vickers has acquired. When shown Vickers' entry in *Who Owns Whom?* they can hardly credit it – 'I've not heard of half these'. Those workers who have been 'taken over' have often had a similar sense of not quite knowing what they're a part of. Some have hoped that it will mark a change for the better:

> We were on a hiding to nothing really. The previous firm was on the way out anyway and the conditions (wages and working conditions I mean) were pretty bad really. Most people hoped that with a big company like Vickers things would work out better all round. It didn't work out like that though.

Taken over – closed down

The first of the major take-overs that took place in the 1960s was that of the old-established firm of office-equipment manufacturers – Roneo. Roneo was attractive to Vickers because of its sales network, and the reputation it had established with government buyers. Important in itself, it also provided Vickers with a marketing outlet for the office furniture which it was already producing as a side-line at Dartford and Crayford.

Before the take-over, Roneo's site at Romford in Essex consisted of three plants: a steel factory which made office machinery such as filing cabinets etc., a print shop which made stencils for duplicators, and a machine factory which made the duplicators themselves. Vickers was obviously concerned to integrate Roneo into its own office machinery division at Dartford, and for two hundred men at Romford this meant redundancy.

The shop stewards' committee at Romford are convinced that the strong shop floor organisation which had been created at the steel factory was a major factor in Vickers' decision. The steel factory employed an all-male labour force with a high proportion of skilled workers. It was these men who demanded recognition of the union from the old Roneo company. In the early 1960s they had struck for two weeks before recognition was granted. As a result of that strike the steel factory became tightly organised. It was there that the toughest piece-work negotiations took place and the wage levels for the rest of the Romford site were set. For Vickers the situation at Dartford seemed much more controllable. So the Romford steel factory would have to close and the Romford men could pick up the pieces of their lives via the dole queue, a job at Ford Dagenham, or a move out of the area. To many it seemed a bad deal. They demonstrated and petitioned but to no avail. Office machinery was to be rationalised.

The closure had a deep effect upon trade unionism at the Romford site. With the workers in the print shop organised separately into the printing unions, the machine factory was left on its own. There the women machinists had only established the beginning of a trade union organisation, and shop stewards now feel that the organisation never recovered from the closure:

> We lost so many good, active trade unionists then. All in one go. They were the militants. They were *the* trade unionists on this site. They had built up an organisation which could set the pace on the site. Vickers had it easy once they were gone.

There were other effects too. Less dramatic perhaps, but important none the less. With the advent of Matthews the shop stewards have noticed a real change in the firm. 'The Vickers crowd', they will tell you, 'believe in paperwork. They sit in the office all day and give orders'. Frequently the contrast is made with the Roneo era, which is fast becoming 'the good old days'. The complaint is that Vickers management don't know the production side of the job:

Some of them come in here, and they haven't got a clue.
They are hydraulics engineers or they worked on submarines –
it's all bloody paperwork with this lot.

The whole nature of the place has changed.

Even though the money was (and still is) worse than at
Ford's, when people came to work at Roneo's they stayed.
The majority of them, when they came in here they'd spend a
life-time here. It was very much a family sort of firm. Uncles,
brothers, sisters, husbands and wives would all work here.
Before Vickers took over it was very close-knit. We've only
moved away from management since Vickers took over. Now
its becoming more like Ford's.

Not all workers in Roneo regret the past in this way. On the Kirby
Estate in Liverpool, Rowe Brothers, a firm which produced office
partitioning, was known as 'a bit of a scab firm' and paid some of the
lowest wages in the area. As a part of the Vickers corporation the
workers there have seen their wages rise considerably. In 1978 a
labourer in the factory earned £57 per week – not much of a wage
perhaps but twice as much as he was earning in 1973! So there are
no regrets on that score. But that's just one part of the story. As at
Romford, take-over has been accompanied by rationalisation – and
in the office equipment division this is now taking place on a
European basis. One of the Kirby workers notes how,

We used to do a lot of exporting from this factory – to the
continent and that sort of thing. But that stopped with this
company because Vickers has a factory in France that has
taken over the market. That was the beginning of the
downturn for this place.

The 'downturn' culminated in the factory's manual labour force
being more than halved in 1976 – a shop floor strength of over one
hundred being reduced to just 45. That was bad enough – but what
is resented more, perhaps, is the way it was accomplished. Again the
'new Vickers' style was revealed:

There had been some voluntary redundancies and at that time
management had said that there would be no further

redundancies – in fact they positively denied that there would be any more. It was only a matter of four weeks when they called another meeting: 'fifty per cent of you are going and that's it' you know. What they said was 'either half go – or all go'.

Another man remembers the events well:

For some time management had been coming down getting all the shop floor together and putting graphs up – 'this is the position, its not too good but we think we're going to pull through and it looks as though we're coming out of the red into the black'. Next thing 'I'm afraid things didn't work out, we're going to try to keep going but its going to mean getting rid of half of you'! That's how they hit us with it. Everyone was stunned really because we thought we were in for another of these graph-type meetings you know.

They read out these names – all the people who were named had to leave the room you know. They were being kept on. Those who were left were for the boot – being made redundant.

The union organisation wasn't too good but there was a shop steward committee and a convenor. All of this committee was included in the redundancies. So they effectively smashed what little union organisation there was there at that time. We've built it up again, and it's better now than it was then – but it was touch and go.

More closures

Crabtree Ltd. a Leeds-based printing machine manufacturer, was taken over by Vickers in 1965. There too the workers had the experience of having their lives cut to fit Vickers' requirements. This time the cost was even greater.

Crabtrees had a factory in London (which had itself been taken over by Crabtrees from Hoe Ltd.) as well as in Leeds and Gateshead. It produced parts for newspaper presses which were completed at Water Lane in Leeds. For Crabtrees this had been a most efficient arrangement. Not so for Vickers. Vickers already had one factory in Leeds (George Manns) and the possibility of another nearby (Dawson, Payne and Lockett Ltd.). The best arrangement for them was to concentrate production in the north. So the Crabtree, Hoe factory in Burrow Road, Peckham – an area badly hit by engineering closedowns generally – was closed down. After a four month fight over 300 people lost their jobs.

The closure of the Hoe factory was part of a general re-organisation of Vickers' printing machinery products so that, as far as possible, production of each product was concentrated in one plant. This was to have serious implications for other plants in the division, in particular the factory at Water Lane. Under Crabtrees, Water Lane had produced two main products, the Sovereign book printing press and the Rotary newspaper press. When work was slack on one product workers could be transferred to another. During the inter-war depression Crabtrees – as Terry Jacques, the ex-convenor, puts it – 'went merrily along with buoyant order books and hardly seemed to suffer from the recession'. But within the Vickers conglomerate this situation was a brake upon profit-ability because it cushioned loss makers. Consequently, production of the Sovereign press was moved to George Mann's.[1]

It could be argued that there is nothing wrong with such rationalisation; that it is a much more efficient and sensible way of organising production, and that similar moves would be made in an economy organised by the workers themselves. Certainly the shop stewards at Water Lane saw the logic in the moves and felt that it would be wrong of them to resist strongly this re-organisation of work:

> George Mann's was in a bit of a poor state then and we had plenty of work. We did object, but if we had gone to any great lengths it would have been really as an attempt to conserve work for ourselves, simply to maintain overtime at the expense of our brothers at Mann's and I like to think we weren't that sort of factory.

But these feelings of brotherhood can all too easily be used against workers in a society dominated not by workers but by the market and corporate power. In such a society, rationalisation also involves control. Rationalisation of product lines makes it easier for the executive at head office to calculate the risks. It frees them from the need to 'carry' loss makers in a particular plant. But it makes the *workers* far more vulnerable. At Water Lane it meant the closure of the plant and large scale redundancies; a decision which (once again) came upon the work force with a sickening suddenness.

At Water Lane the shop stewards committee carefully monitored the job situation in the factory, comparing on a monthly basis the numbers who left and the numbers recruited. In the summer of 1973 their records started to show a gradual increase in the numbers of those who were not replaced. They asked questions. The answers they got were merely denials that any serious trend was building up 'not the sort of answers you could make a fuss about, not the sort that indicated anything serious was amiss'.

Then a small, but completely unprecedented, incident occurred which aroused their suspicions. One man was recruited and given a starting date. Before he took up his job at Crabtree he received a letter saying that 'due to the economic circumstances' the company would have to rescind the offer of employment. At the same time a vacancy for a personnel manager was not filled and the production manager took on 'personnel' duties. A funny business. If a personnel manager wasn't necessary maybe 'the personnel' would soon be gone too. The shop stewards' suspicions were confirmed when Vickers stopped all recruitment because of lack of orders. A major French order that would have provided three or four years' work had just been lost. The loss fitted into a more general trend.

The shop stewards committee decided to ban overtime. But redundancies were taking place even before they sensed something was seriously wrong. The stewards had 'allowed' 120 men to be made redundant over a period of ten to twelve months. As they argued: 'The work was not there; we could see it was not there.' There was no sign of new orders for Rotary newspaper presses. Major changes had taken place in the technology of newspaper printing and Vickers had not kept up with these changes. Crabtrees' Rotary press was the Rolls Royce of newspaper printing machines. There was no mass production involved: each press was built according to customer specifications. But by the mid-1960s a mass-produced newspaper printing press – a newspaper version of the web-fed press – had been developed and was being sold at far lower prices than the traditional Rotary presses.

The shop stewards at Water Lane were not informed of the seriousness of the situation. Neither were they told that Vickers had decided to discontinue production of web-fed presses. This was nothing new, and for some time the committee had subscribed to *Printing News* in order to get information (especially on technological changes) which management would not divulge. On 17 October 1975 they read the headlines – 'No more web-fed presses: shock decision by Vickers'. It was quite a shock. The stewards played hell with management, who responded with an ambiguous denial. While they agreed that orders were low they declared emphatically that the factory's future was not in jeopardy. However on their first day back after Christmas the workers at Water Lane were told that the major part of the plant would be closed. Eighteen months before the closure 800 men worked at Water Lane; the closure left just 125 behind.

Why was the closure so sudden? It seems that at some point along the line senior management at Millbank – the bankers – decided that the risks involved in developing the new technologies necessary to produce the cheaper web-fed presses did not justify the investment.[2] In spite of the talk of business 'risk', Vickers had never taken any risks at Water Lane. Most of the investment that had been made in the plant was provided by the government. The main fact is that Vickers was determined to concentrate its power upon its more secure lines and (with an eye on the property market) to eventually close the Water Lane factory. But the workers at Water Lane could not be told of this. Advance warning might have given them the time to prepare effective resistance. Water Lane had to be kept open until the last order was squeezed out, until the workforce there had produced the last pound of profit for Vickers. And then closure. Just three months before it happened it was being denied as a possibility, and potential customers were still being contacted.

After all this the people still working for Crabtree Vickers in Leeds – at the Hunslet works and what remains of Water Lane – do not feel very secure. They now operate as a single Leeds works. The empty factories at Water Lane have been taken over by Vickers' property company ready to be rented or sold. Rumour has it that the Leeds works have been given two years to become profitable. After considerable losses in 1977 the prospects are not good.

The closure of Water Lane illustrates very sharply the extent of the control which a centralised senior management in a multi-plant, multi-product company exercised over the overall development of the company.[3]

It could be argued that centralised power is only occasionally exercised in such an extreme form. Vickers' policy of giving plant management responsibility for the profitability of its unit of production can, in good times, give the impression that the local management are in control. But when the market is less certain this autonomy wears thin. The movement of products, running down of jobs, and sub-contracting, all of which accompany the rationalisation of product, indicate to the workers that their destiny is out of their hands.

An uncertain future

This sense of powerlessness is especially acute in small plants like the bottle machinery plant in Thetford, Norfolk. Vickers took over the plant as part of Dawson Barfos in 1973. Since the take-over the plant has experienced the same sort of rationalisation that took place in the printing machinery division. Products have been moved to other parts of the Packaging Division (the valve speed gear, they guess, has gone to Crayford, sterilisers to Gomersal and so on) and at the same time they have seen a regular flow of men leaving, not to be replaced. In the last year the shopfloor workforce had declined by 20 per cent.

To the workers at Thetford it looks as if Vickers treat the plant as the place where products can be tried out and the job timings and production processes established – in short as the experimental and odd-job plant for the rest of the packaging division. The fact they are working on a new product, a fast bottle filler (the LA12), does not dispel these feelings. They have seen how

> Sometimes management get over all the problems of producing a new machine at a plant where the wages are low and then once they've got the times all worked out it is put somewhere where the wages are high.

And they've no guarantee it could not be done again with the LA12.

What is left is a strong sense of insecurity and demoralisation. One shop steward describes this feeling:

> When you go round talking to people about, for example, the pensions scheme, they're not interested. They're not talking about five or six years' time, they're saying 'I wonder whether we'll be closed down, how much redundancy money will we get'.

It would be wrong to see all this as a single consequence of size. People at Thetford (like those at Kirby Partitions and many of the other small plants taken over in these years) had no love for the old regime. In fact they talk of the time when they awaited the take-over by Vickers with high expectations. 'Perhaps someone will come and sort this place out.' Thetford was sorted out by locating it within a division of a major corporation. The people who work there have lost out to the extent that their lives are now fitted into the accounting logic of that world. But daily, at their place of work 'the same idiots are still there' – people are bossed around and insulted. For them the take-over produced few gains.

Chapter 6

Run-Down

While most of the 'old Vickers' has been nationalised, parts of it still remain. On Tyneside – where the company originated along the banks of the river during the last century – the old Elswick and Scotswood works still operate along with others that have been acquired since the war. But whereas Vickers employed near 20,000 workers in these two plants alone in 1945, the entire manual labour force on the Tyne (and this in six factories) has been reduced to a quarter of this total. At Scotswood, where thousands once found employment, just seven hundred and fifty work today. Elswick too has declined, and the works which was once the engineering centre of the company now employs just two thousand men in three divisions.

The consequences of Vickers' run-down have been deep and far reaching for Tyneside. It is important to appreciate that Vickers has for most of this century been the biggest employer of skilled engineering workers on Tyneside. Situated north of the river in West Newcastle, the Vickers' works provided one of the main apprenticeship schemes for boys in the area. In 1976, by way of contrast, they started just thirty school leavers in the apprentice school. While not as clear an example of a company town as Barrow in Furness, the significance of Vickers to the social fabric of West Newcastle has been a profound one. Vickers' decline has coincided with the transformation of the Benwell locality into an 'inner city area' – the current euphemism for an area of high unemployment and physical decay.

In this situation people's emotions and feelings run deep, and they are often tinged with ambiguity. They talk of the past:

Newcastle used to be a canny town. There used to be all sorts down this end but it's all gone now. It's changed out of

recognition. It's like Vickers. This used to be a good firm one
time. It had the best apprenticeship in the area. If you'd been
trained at Vickers you could get a job anywhere in Newcastle.
But there's no apprentices now.

A local union official notes that Vickers Ltd. is 'one of the hardest
and most reactionary employers to deal with on this river. Without
a doubt. They're a tough outfit.' At a joint shop stewards meeting of
all the Tyneside plants one steward said how he'd

worked for Vickers for 42 years and I've had enough of them.
I hate Vickers and all it stands for. I'm sick to death of them.
I hate all that they've been getting away with over these years.
I really want to have a go at this company. They have been
getting away with murder in this company.

A tough situation, then, in one of the homes of engineering trade
union and shop steward organisation. Let's look at the Tyneside
run-down more closely.

Odd-jobbing at Scotswood

In 1976, Lord Robens, speaking as the chairman of Vickers Ltd.,
claimed that the engineering side of the company was 'now on a
firm basis in the United Kingdom and the prospects for 1976 are
good for most group trading activities'. Having given the good
news he went on to add, ominously, that 'orders for heavy
engineering products slackened at the start of the year'. For the
workers at the Scotswood works this seemed like another example
of the double-talk they had experienced over the years. In the 25
years that the works has been in decline the men have produced a
long – almost bewildering – series of products. A shop steward
remembers a few of them:

First you had locomotives. Locomotives was the main heavy
engineering product here before the war (in fact if you go
over the main fly-over way and look over the river you can
see the outline of the paint marks where it says *Vickers
Locomotives* on the edge of the shop). And then during the
war the guns. Then you had the tractors, then the power presses,
then the Standard Telephone and Cable work and now

they're diversifying into this baler because the presses are still at a low ebb. And we're doing a hell of a lot of sub-contract work. All the time we're moving around. We're never had a product at Scotswood. Not a product there has been a market for. It's a case of moving around, chopping and changing all the time.

Scotswood is the clearest example of the legacy of Vickers' military past. Relying basically upon war for its market the company filled up spare capacity in peace time with odd-jobbing – orders picked up on the fringes of the market. Plants like Scotswood were essentially jobbing shops: among the biggest in the world, no doubt, but in its essentials (reliance upon an intermittent supply of odd jobs) just that. This was the basis of its vulnerability. Vickers has been unable to compete with continental capital goods manufacturers (making the machines that make the machines) and their highly capitalised and specialised factories.

There was in fact just one attempt to establish Scotswood as more than a jobbing shop. Scott, the company's official historian, writes that in 1945, the factory was seen to be a 'a first class works, and the company was anxious to make use of it.' A major investment programme was set up to convert the Sherman tank into the Shervik tractor and plans were laid for a £10 million turnover in tractor production. However these plans came unstuck in the face of American competition and the arrival of a lighter four-wheel design. The scheme was closed down and 900 men were sacked. (Many of the workers are still convinced that the full story of this debacle has never been told.) For those who remained the scheme and the 'old Scotswood Works' remains a memory:

A lot of Scotswood has been knocked down. The tractor shop: it was a massive place. That's when I first came here to take up my apprenticeship. I started my time off in the tractor shop. The shop was a quarter of a mile long. There was one bay; you went in the door and when you got to the end you'd walked a quarter of a mile, well that's warehouses now. Where that car park is at the top it used to be a great big mains store. There were the smaller shops that's warehouses now, and that area by the jetty – there used to be

shops there too. And other little shops here and there. Even
the offices – they were a lot bigger than they are now.

The failure of the tractor scheme (for Scott 'a venturesome
departure which failed') seemed to have taught the 'service
element' at Vickers a lot about the commercial world. From then on
they decided to play it safe with Scotswood – to carry on odd-
jobbing with the existing machinery and workforce. But in a world
where safety comes only to those who can sell, there is no stability in
leaving things as they are. 'Stability' comes from 'forward planning', investment and market research – without this companies
face a steady decline. As Vickers played safe, the living standards
and lives of the workforce at Scotswood became more and more
dependent upon the orders that could be picked up around the
edges of the market. As the market expanded and contracted so
were men hired or laid off. In 1969 there was 'a sudden rush of
orders' and an extra 200 men were taken on. Two years later came a
drop in orders and 215 were paid off. The following year there were
more redundancies. Increasingly Scotswood could not compete –
even in the jobbing market.

Their telecommunications orders, for example, originally ran to
20 sets a week; now they are down to two, and for the men who work
there the reason for this decline is clear:

> For that type of product to compete with everybody you've
> got to have modern type of equipment and machinery . . .
> They have that fine a tolerance or they're not accepted:
> there's not got to be a scratch on the job or nowt . . . This
> factory has *never* invested any money in the machinery for
> this product.

Elswick and the decline of armaments

The Elswick works – Vickers' oldest and major plant in the area –
has had a similar history since the war. Today just two thousand
men work there making tanks in the, renamed, 'Defence Systems
Division', body pressings for the car industry, and a wide range of
non-ferrous products. The decline of Elswick can be closely related
to the decline in armaments production, a decline which the shop
steward committee has supported: 'You know we've said to the

members. You're socialists aren't you. Jobs for armaments! Come on you should be welcoming this opportunity of getting out of the war business.'

What they didn't support – or see to be at all necessary – was a decline in engineering production at the works. Like Scotswood, the men at Elswick have worked on an almost endless list of products, and like the Scotswood men too they have a story to tell about every product that was 'lost' or taken away from Elswick. The talk is of deals, of mistakes, of MPs and officials, of who said what to whom, of trains to London . . .

A variable speed gear (VSG) was once produced at Elswick, until it was closed down in 1959. Prior to the closure, part of the work had been moved to Weymouth. The shop stewards committee supported the move at the time – because they thought it made sense: 'Well it was Labour party policy at the time you see. Move things to areas of seasonal unemployment. That made sense to us. We weren't faced with any dramatic redundancies so it made sense – work sharing like.' Again, like the workers at Water Lane, they were to realise that you need the power to back up the things which you think of as sensible. The closure at Elswick was followed by the closure of Weymouth, followed by the concentration and rationalisation of work at South Marston.

Another big project that came and went from Elswick was 'the die shop' which produced the die that stamped metal into car bodies. It was a new project with new technology, producing in a highly competitive market. Vickers safeguarded the project by recruiting some of its best tool fitters – 'there were really good tradesmen in the die shop, they brought a lot in from Scotswood' – and subjecting them to maximum supervision. Repetitive work, high tolerances, one supervisor to fifteen men . . . it had all the elements of a pressurised situation. And it proved to be an explosive one.

The work was terrible in the die shop but a great solidarity grew up there, you know. The pressure was tremendous – we got through four production managers there. At one point they were talking about bringing in a lot of Sunderland foremen – to break up the solidarity, you know. But it was good. We had quite a lot of social functions and in the shop itself we established total control on flexibility and overtime. You know, we had a lot of walk outs. The works convenor was always down to get you to act reasonable. The solidarity was good – it came out of the situation we were in.

The solidarity of the die shop men had to be broken. Their control over the workshop was challenged by management and the result was a strike which lasted ten weeks. One of the shop stewards remembers:

We were out for ten weeks that time. And we won. We got no backing from the rest of the works but we won. People were doing all sorts of things during the strike. A lot of people had ice cream vans! We had a really well organised strike committee, and a lot of lads who really knew the town you know. It was difficult to get them back to work in the end!

They won the strike but the die shop closed down. And without the die shop, the VSG or commercial engineering (which was moved to Scotswood), or the naval work (which moved to Barrow), or the printing presses (which moved to Leeds) Elswick's run-down continued. It remains a viable, profitable operation only in as much as its future (and the future of the workers there) is tied to the sub-contracted order of Chieftain tanks that the company receives from the ordnance factories. For all their hopes, socialists at Elswick are still in the war-production business.

Halting the run-down

This overall pattern of decline is a central feature of Vickers' operations on Tyneside. While a detailed consideration of 'the trade union response' must wait until the next chapter, we can at this point record one successful check which workers have made upon the rapid loss of jobs in the Vickers' factories.

In 1977 the workers at the Scotswood works were informed that the company would be making a further 150 men redundant. This time, the shop stewards committee decided that they had had enough and that there was no way that the redundancies were going to be accepted.

We just decided that we were not going to take it. We told
management clearly that we weren't accepting it. And we told
some of our own members too. People started talking and
asking about redundancy money. 'We're not entertaining any
redundancy in this works.'

This resolve to fight, was heightened by a feeling that, one way or
another, they had been taken for a ride by Vickers Ltd. They
complained of never being given sufficient information and of
being kept constantly in the dark over the company's future plans.
They had a strong feeling that 'on a lot of these things – the big ones
especially – the plans are made by Vickers House well in advance of
it coming off'. They suspected too that slight dips in the market
were used by management to enforce 'cost cutting' that couldn't be
achieved when order-books were full. And more than anything they
felt that management had had things pretty much its own way on all
these issues.

In the 1950s the trade union organisation in the factory had – if
anything – been slower than Vickers in reacting to the new post-war
situation. And then, after the 1975 Redundancy Payments Act, a
workforce with a high proportion of older workers – who were given
the first choice of any redundancy money – did not provide a strong
basis for a militant anti-redundancy campaign. The shop stewards
are sure however that

If people had done something positive about it earlier
they could have solved the situation. Anyway now the
situation has gone too far. We can't accept redundancies now.
People think they can leave and get another job. But where
can they get another job in this area? There's no jobs here,
man. And if we lose another hundred and fifty jobs at
Scotswood that's those jobs less in the area. We're just going
to have to get cracking and get something organised.

By 1977 unemployment was a major issue on Tyneside. The
declining heavy engineering markets that were affecting Vickers
were being felt throughout the local area. The effects crystalised
first at another local heavy engineering firm – C. A. Parsons. At
Parsons, the workers and their shop stewards had organised a
campaign against redundancies at the plant and in the region

generally. Within the plant they had set up a 'corporate committee' made up of all grades within the factory; they organised a march which was joined by men from Scotswood, who then discussed the idea of establishing a 'corporate committee' of their own to discuss and negotiate the future of the factory with management. This committee questioned management's investment plans, the problems of future orders, and of new product lines for the factory. The committee publicised its activity via a meeting with the local council and telegrams to MPs and to Vickers House. It received strong support from other shop steward committees within Vickers – particularly those on Tyneside. Today members of the committee are convinced that this publicity and the unity reflected in the corporate committee gave Vickers the message that redundancies were to be resisted this time and ensured that work was moved from other parts of the company to Scotswood.

> Work came from Barrow, work came from South Marston, work came from Dawson (the 'mousetraps' came from there) and work is coming from Elswick. Work which apparently wasn't there before. But its always been there. If we hadn't got organised here it would have stayed there.

As a jobbing shop the workforce at Scotswood were able to pressurise for a share in the work that was around. But this work-sharing is very much a short term reprieve (one which, incidentally, was communicated to the shop stewards and the corporate committee through the office grapevine and not officially by management), a reprieve that was dependant upon other plants having reasonably full order-books. Within the modern Vickers, work-sharing offers no really viable long term solution for Scotswood. To survive in the multinational world in the long term, Scotswood will have to be rebuilt. And this raises another aspect of the union campaign. As a result of the pressure placed upon management, the shop stewards on the corporate committee were given access to 'the secret room'. It turned out that behind a door at Scotswood, which has only one key, there was a full scale model of a new Scotswood plant, that had been lying there, locked away, for the past eighteen months. A model that *may* become the reality of a new Scotswood, depending on the calculations of the banker at head office.

One thing workers at Scotswood *can* be certain of is that the future of the plant is up for grabs. It has no indefinite future as a jobbing shop. The low rate of investment and the diminishing design team are seriously reducing its ability to squeeze further orders out of the increasingly competitive heavy engineering market. This market is such that even with a higher rate of investment the future would be very uncertain. The scale of investment required for heavy engineering products and the slow rate of turnover make it virtually impossible for single companies to carve out a niche, especially now that developing countries are establishing capital goods industries of their own. European co-ordination is becoming the order of the day in heavy engineering as in other major industries. Scotswood has been allowed to run down to the point that only a complete rebuilding and re-equipping would give it a future in these conditions. But there are no trends in Vickers recent past to indicate that management is likely to spend the millions required to establish Scotswood in this slow and precarious market.

Chapter 7

Developed

A large part of the experience which workers have had of the 'new Vickers' is contained in the insecurity that has come with run down and rationalisation. However, Vickers has also invested a lot of money in fixed capital resources. New plants *have* been built and profitable lines developed and marketed. What has been the workers' experience of this 'development' under Vickers?

In the accounting logic of the 'Matthew System' – a system which is simply the internal expression of the wider corporate economy – investment is related to returns, to profit. 'Development' therefore is dependent upon certain conditions being met, both within the factory and the market. Hence the detailed calculations that go into assessing production costs, market share and the like.

Two of Vickers sites – at South Marston and Crayford – have been the beneficiaries of new investment programmes. And at both, the company was concerned to extract 'the right conditions' out of the workforce. South Marston is a major site in the Vickers empire. It is the headquarters of the Engineering Group and as such it has its own private airfield from which the chairman of the group, Jim Hendin, flies a company plane to all the outlying sites. It is also the home of some of Vickers future money spinners, such as Design and Procurement[1] and the Nuclear Division, both of which, incidentally, employ very few production workers.

The site is located on the outskirts of Swindon in Wiltshire, a town whose industrial base was built around railway engineering and, later, aircraft production. Soon after the nationalisation and 'rationalisation' of the railways, most of the railway engineering was moved away to Derby. Then in the mid 1950s with the re-organisation of the aircraft industry, aircraft production was moved to Weybridge and Bristol. At Swindon, as on Tyneside and elsewhere, rationalisation and re-organisation was linked with loss of jobs. The apprenticeship scheme was cut from around 80 to less than 15. (On the South Marston site the training school building is now used by a paint company, and the boys' training is carried out in an annexe of the canteen.) As with apprenticeships, so with jobs generally: the 1950 workforce of around 3000 has been cut back to 620.

Nevertheless it is clear that South Marston has been one of the beneficiaries of Vickers' re-organisation. The loss of aircraft production was partly compensated for by the concentration on the site of all of Vickers' hydraulic production. As one shop steward puts it:

> Management intended that South Marston should be built up into one of the major Vickers plants. They promised us that they intended to double or treble the workforce. They talked about a new shop for the hydraulics division. All sorts of ambitious plans were put to the stewards' committee. But all we had was condensing, not expansion.

The development at South Marston depended upon getting the balance right. Part of the problem was old plant and equipment, part the mix of hydraulic products which was no longer appropriate for the market. A further problem for management was lack of 'discipline' on the shop floor and inadequate managerial control over production. Management had tried on various occasions in the past to introduce procedures which would impose discipline on workers in the hydraulics division, but success was only partial. They had also tried unsuccessfully to introduce elements of a data control system.

To deal with this situation Vickers introduced a new management team in the mid 1970s who offered a five year plan as a solution. This plan offered the workers investment (a loan from the bank, as it were) on the condition of good behaviour – a new-style productivity deal in which the future of the site (new buildings and machinery) was traded for new production methods, better work discipline and greater individual responsibility. And to keep an eye on the smooth running of the whole process the company would introduce a fully computerised production control system, to be operated through the Management Services Division in New-castle.

Many of the stewards had doubts about the whole deal. They were sceptical about what guarantee they would have of the company keeping its side of the bargain. As one steward pointed out in 1977, 'Investment can be a very nebulous notion: there's been a lot of planning but no doing. Nothing has materialised. No money has been invested up to this point in time, although the building plans have been changed on at least three occasions'.

Some workers feel that many negotiating levers may have been lost by accepting a single 'job lot'. There is also concern over the effects of numerically controlled machinery – the product of new investment – on manning levels. Under the five year plan the work force should be kept at approximately present levels, and stewards are concerned about the possibility of this 'approximate' being downgraded in the future. But mostly they felt – and still feel – that they had no option. They felt that there was no basis upon which they could have challenged the 'take it or leave it' deal they were offered. For them, and the South Marston workforce, planning with strings had become the price of a job.

The workers at Vickers Crayford factory in London have been through a similar experience. During the war and into the late 1950s Crayford and the nearby Dartford works had been producers of guns, director gears and other highly complex machines. In a search for replacements a variety of different machines – for paint manufacture, for bottle filling, for cable insulating and twisting, and so on – were produced one after another. Crayford, an old factory with high running costs, was in the jobbing business. A business which couldn't last:

You can see the old factory – the remnants of it. It covers a vast area. Now we've come to what we call an oversized garage. They're always talking about expansion but this is old hat as far as we're concerned. All that's happened is that we've got smaller and smaller. The run down happened bit by bit. I've been involved in no end of redundancies — the worst thing the Labour government did was to introduce the Redundancy Payment Act. People forget to fight for their jobs. Now everybody has got a price.

The run-down ended when the workers were told that the factory would have to close. Immediately, however, local management insisted that there was a future with a new factory producing a new product (a drum metric conversion unit) for which there was thought to be a strong US market. The workforce organised a campaign to save jobs at Crayford, exerting pressure on politicians and Millbank Tower. In the end the works was saved: 'There was a hell of a fight went on. We went to Whitehall twice to get the new factory open. We say it was these trips that did it. The managing director says it was because of his recommendation.'

In deciding to overturn the earlier decision the accountants at Millbank said that they were impressed by the financial case that had been put to them, but that they had been finally persuaded by the 'team spirit' which management and workers showed in their campaign. Crayford had proven a suitable place to invest. Two million pounds were forthcoming from the banker but the manual worker 'team' would need to be cut. In the end 620 of them started work, although the promise had been for many more. As it was, a works employing 13,000 workers in 1950 had been cut back to 'a garage'.

> The managing director said that we had to be grateful that
> Vickers put £2 million into it . . . But we never got to know
> anything about what they did with the money they got when
> they sold off the old factory. They sold off part of our sports
> ground. It was denied they were selling it and then there was
> a notice in the paper that it had been sold for £1.5 million.
> We argued it was our factory, we'd developed it. All the riches
> were ours. But no – when they sold it the money just
> disappeared, to the London office we must assume.

And so even in this successful plant, which has all the signs of expansion and none of the run-down atmosphere of Scotswood, the workforce have little confidence in their future. They have learnt that even a new factory and a new product are not a guarantee of very much. As it was, the main new product virtually fell through. The new factory had been laid out for it, but the expected market collapsed. Nobody knew why. All they know is that Crayford ended up depending on one product, a stitching machine, and making spares for bottling machinery. And the packaging industry is changing, too: from glass bottles to cans and plastic containers, from cardboard boxes needing stitching machines to polythene bags needing completely different machinery. People can see these changes going on and they know that they will be affected by them, but they can't control them: they don't get to know of company plans until the decisions are made, and, as one steward put it 'things just creep up on you'.

The signs of expansion, advertisements for labour and so on, do not give the Crayford workers confidence. That really only comes from having some control over your future, and be their plant successful or running down, the one thing all workers in Vickers have in common is this lack of control. Here in Crayford it makes them wary of change. As one of the stewards put it, 'With Vickers the only future you can see is three months, or the length of time in which you can be made redundant.' And another, 'The whole atmosphere at Vickers is "how long before somebody says you're no longer necessary".'

Chapter 8

The Paradox
of Modernisation

The story of Vickers' progress since the war appears in a different light now than it did earlier on in this book. In fact, with all the chaos that has resulted it is a wonder that it can be called progress at all. Clearly 'modernising' isn't all that it appears to be. Part of the problem here is that in spite of all the changes – the centralisation, the increased profit consciousness, the new investment – basic things have remained the same. There has been no change in the *purpose* of production. Vickers has always been concerned with making profit, only the circumstances have changed since the war. Vickers has always been run by bosses who give orders, who tell people what to do, who *decide* things: there are new managers at Vickers but they remain the same in this respect.

This constancy within change is the central paradox of the modernisation of Vickers. It is reflected in many aspects of the company's operations. No more so than in the coexistence of sophisticated technological advances (the product of human labour and intelligence) with urban devastation, large scale unemployment and the chronic tedium that makes up the working lives of the majority.

Technological advance

The reporting of technological change and development is often done through the vista of 'Tomorrow's World': technical problems are presented with technical solutions – any 'social problems' are either ignored or thought to be solved almost incidentally and by the way. But things are a good deal more complicated than this. To begin with it cannot be assumed that technological change and the introduction of advanced technological processes will automatically produce better conditions for the men and women who work the factories. At the Howson Algraphy plant in Leeds (which is probably the most profitable of all Vickers' operations) lithographic plates are produced by continuous automatic processes. This technology gives Vickers' an immense lead in the industry and the workers are glad of the present stability of employment which comes from it. However they have had to suffer the major consequences of continuous production as their bodies adjust to the continental shift system. As the machines run so must the men; day in, day out, light or dark. Two days, two afternoons, three nights, two off, two days, three afternoons, two nights . . .

Recently we've heard a lot of talk about what is fashionably called 'jet lag', the disturbance to physical and mental performance caused by flying across time-zones. In experimental simulations of the London to Japan time shift, subjects lost seven per cent of their muscular strength and five per cent in central nervous system efficiency . . .

Jet lag is just a short taste of what its like to be on [shifts], but without the dreary surroundings of a factory at night and in circumstances when mistakes can cost only money – not life or limb. Shift lag is an altogether more serious condition. It affects you every day, every week, every year, for the rest of your working life – if you can stick it.

Patrick Kinnersly, *The Hazards of Work*, Pluto 1974

Shift work – and an intensification of the stress involved in factory life – is one consequence of advanced production techniques. Another is the danger and risks involved in the increasingly widespread utilisation of toxic substances within manufacturing industry. The Slingsby Sailplanes plant at Kirkby Moorside in

Yorkshire produces fibreglass mini-submarines, as well as gliders, and naval furniture. Vickers Slingsby (as it is now known) is, to quote the *Engineer*,

> synonymous with highly sophisticated glass reinforced plastics technology. Its reputation as a leading authority in its use of structural composite materials stems from applications . . . as diverse as gliders, airships, shipfittings and deep water submersibles. (23 March 1978)

This article went on to point out that:

> At current prices the bare cost of making the LR5 is put at around £500,000. However, allowing for spares and certification after sub-sea trials, the final cost comes to nearer £1 million. The cost of hiring a submersible with diving crew and support ship is now about £20,000 a day.

The March issue of *Vickers News* carried a similar story, together with an account of a visit to the plant by Lord Robens, Sir Peter Matthews and the local MP. The headline read: 'Their products range from the skies to the ocean depths' and readers were told how,

> Vickers-Slingsby's range of expertise was demonstrated to MP's and journalists when the division held its first-ever open day this month. During the tour round the busy works, visitors were able to see for themselves the many specialised products built on the edges of the Yorkshire Moors. (23 March 1978)

Neither story touched upon the experiences of the workers who make these amazing pieces of equipment. If they had, the contrast would have been acute.

Fibreglass production is full of health hazards: it involves working with resins which can cause throat infections and skin diseases; it involves working with dust as dangerous as asbestos; it also involves working in an atmosphere of styrene fumes. Generally, fibreglass production involves working on a site surrounded by toxic substances and fumes. Workers at Slingsby had never expected the previous owner to show much concern for their welfare. But from 'a big firm like Vickers' they hoped for different treatment, especially as Lord Robens had served as chairman of the

Crane firr
fined £85(

Fall derailed packed train

A TYNESIDE engineering firm yesterday was fined £850.

One of its cranes toppled across a railway line in the path of a packed passenger train.

The accident, which led to six people being hurt and 200 others escaping injury, was inevitable, Newcastle magistrates were told yesterday.

Weight

The day the overloaded crane crumpled across the tracks and an early-morning commuter train ploughed into the wreckage was recounted to city magistrates.

Under the Health and Safety at Work Act, the company had put members of the public at risk by the badly - conducted lifting operation, she said.

Vickers Ltd. were fined £300 for using a crane not properly maintained; £200 for its being loaded over the safety limit; £200 for a badly conducted lifting operation; and £150 for the crane not being examined regularly.

The firm pleaded guilty

government committee on 'Health and Safety at Work'. The final report of this committee had argued that

> Promotion of safety and health at work is an essential function of good management . . . The boardroom has the influence, power and resources to take initiatives and to set the pattern . . . the cue will be taken from the top . . . If directors and senior managers are unable to find time to take a positive interest in safety and health, it is unrealistic to suppose that this will not adversely affect the attitudes and performance of junior managers, supervisors and employees on the shop floor.

Judged by these standards the Vickers board comes out of the situation at Slingsby very badly indeed.

At Slingsby the workers insist that until they organised themselves into a union through UCATT management took little or no responsibility for the health hazards involved in everyday working conditions at the plant. On one occasion they showed management an article in the *Yorkshire Post* which said that fibreglass should be classed with asbestos from a health point of view. The article said that working with fibreglass without sufficient protection could cause cancer. A number of books on health and safety at work argued the same point. The stewards described how management said this was 'a load of rubbish'. They tell of the time when,

> Three years ago we asked for a simple straightforward medical test to be done yearly at the firm's expense; a chest x-ray and so on, so that the firm would have a monitoring system of what was going on. Management turned round and said that 'your health is your responsibility'. Their comment was 'if you think it's dangerous, if you don't like working here, you know what to do'.

On one occasion an inspector came to the plant and found that the fire bell could not be heard by men who were using a compressed air tool for trimming – and this in a factory full of substances which tend to ignite spontaneously. The workers and their stewards are concerned over this fire hazard. While maintenance staff carry out weekly tests of the automatic sprinkler system and all departments carry copies of the procedure to be followed in the case of fire, no fire drill has ever been organised. The stewards are particularly worried by this, as they are about the kind of medical facilities which Vickers make available: at Slingsby the medical staff is rudimentary. The workers have tried, unsuccessfully, to get a shower put in, in case anyone got peroxide hardener on them. They asked for that three years ago. Technological advance clearly provides no guarantee that the safety – and general interests – of the workers will be catered for.

Automation and jobs

Modern technological processes are having an increasingly important and general effect upon factory life. Automated machinery marks a real advance in human ingenuity. It could provide the possibility of freeing people from routine labour and extending their own creative capacities. In practice, however, the introduction and use of such machinery almost always seems to have achieved the opposite effect.

The machinery that is particularly important here are the numerically-controlled (NC) and computer-numerically-controlled (CNC) machine tools which are now being introduced rapidly into British engineering shops, replacing the traditional manually operated borers, millers, grinders, drills and lathes that make up skilled engineering work. At Vickers the company's chairman made it clear that,

> We have to automate. The workers know this too. They want
> new machines. A firm that doesn't introduce NC machines
> will go out of business. You see these machines, once they are
> set, they will go on producing and the 10,000th component
> will be the same as the first one. You have much greater
> accuracy, greater output and greater quality. And the quality
> is very important because it leads to better assembly at the
> various points in the production process. So we have to have
> these machines and whenever there is money to spare,
> another quarter of a million pounds, we buy another machine
> tool.

Automation is here to stay then, and it is worth noting initially that it is taking place within workshops that employ high proportions of skilled workers. It is skilled work (and not the burdensome and monotonous labouring and 'semi-skilled' work) which is being automated. To quote Christensen:

In a couple of cases where NC machines were operated by skilled workers there had been complaints of boredom owing to the long periods of inactivity while the machines were actually running, but, possibly because of the newness of most of the installations, complaints of frustration caused by constant attention and anxiety to prevent snags and breakdowns outnumbered complaints of boredom by about ten to one.

Erik Christensen, *Labour Research Department Survey of Firms*, 1968

Skilled manual employees in most plants said that job satisfaction in the industry was declining. There seemed to be two main reasons for this. The first was the effect on production techniques of increased standardisation which led to longer runs and made possible the introduction of flowline assembly methods. Secondly the introduction of numerically-controlled machines has led to a loss of skill on the shop floor in many plants. Tapes were prepared mainly in the office and this removed much of the skill element from the operator's job.

NEDO interviews, *NEDO Report*, April 1976

In the early days there had been some resistance to NC machines. This is no longer the case. The unions took a money negotiating attitude to any problems. No significant industrial relations problems had been experienced after this early phase. But there are problems of job satisfaction. If they can, they recruit skilled people to operate NC machines since they have to pay them skilled rate anyway. Skilled men get bored on all NC machines. They need to control machines. Before, the machine would only work with them there. Now, they only have marginal control.

N Sword and P Senkes, *Brighton Survey*, 1978

The difficulty of giving people meaningful employment has overtaken housing as the nations' most important social issue.

Dr Graham Lomas, General Secretary of London Council of Social Services 1976

Programme control systems were designed to control machines capable of producing a wide range of articles in different sizes and shapes (and to produce only a few of each type) faster and more cheaply than by conventional methods. This was achieved by fitting standard multi-purpose machines with an electronic or electro-mechanical control system capable of receiving information about the movements required of the machine to produce any component, and of translating the information into the required movements in the machine's positioning system. All previous types of automation had relied on designing the machines to fixed dimensions and speeds, thus doing away with human control over the manufacture of a narrow range of articles only.

In other words programme-controlled machines are designed to perform the role of a skilled craftsman engaged in batch production.[1]

The numerically-controlled machinery operates on a principle similar to that of the player piano in which a tune is 'programmed' on to holes on a paper roll, and the holes, as they move round, activate the piano keys to produce the programmed tune. In a numerically-controlled machine, a control unit with a punched tape device controlling the tool according to numerical measurements, and a monitoring device, originate signals which activate power drives controlling the work, tool, coolant etc. Thus the cutting, boring, milling etc. take place according to the programme. The crucial feature of this process is that the conceptualisation and calculation involved in a job is separated from the machining. The technical advantages of NC machinery were made clear in the AUEW *Journal* by Dan Sharpe, convenor of Vickers' machine tool plant, KTM:

The time and skill required can be substantially reduced with numerical control because numerical control takes away the multi-operational category to a one machine job, reduces handling time and the skill required, and often produces a better quality component with fewer rejects.[2]

The same point was put in a different way by Braverman in his book *Labor and Monopoly Capital*.

Complex metal cutting . . . slow and demanding when the calculations are made in the course of cutting, may be coded with relative ease and cut with assurance . . . once coded a job need never be analysed again; the tape may be kept on file and used whenever a remake is called for. The processes of metal cutting are virtually automatic, relieving the worker of the need for close control of the machine while cutting is in progress. The separation of conceptualisation and calculation from the machine means that the tool itself is in more constant use for metal cutting; at the same time, it goes through its continuous cutting path without interruption, which also makes for more efficient use of these expensive pieces of equipment.[3]

This process has been further revolutionised by the development of computer circuitry based on silicone chip microprocessors. The pocket calculator is one sign of this advance; another (as we shall see in a moment) is the prospect of the automated factory.

British industry was in fact slow to invest in this kind of hardware, Christensen estimates that in 1960,

only a handful of programmed machine tools had been installed in Britain, and only a couple of them could be found outside manufacturers' research departments and the workshops of higher education institutions. The first installations of NC for naval production appear to have been made in 1956–57 . . . the total number of machine tools fitted with NC installed by December 1962 [were] 232, and from January 1963 up to the end of March 1964 another 163 were installed.

In the last few years it appears that investment in NC machining has increased quite rapidly. To quote Dan Sharpe again,

There appear to be signs now that British industrialists are realigning their thinking on the prospect of numerically-controlled machine tools . . . Possibly they see large sections of the manufacturing industry going the same way as the motor cycle industry unless they can compete with world markets.

A recent survey of NC and CNC utilisation conducted by the Department of Engineering Products at the University of Birmingham revealed that 50 per cent of the sampled firms employed over 10 NC machines (25 per cent over 20) and at least one CNC machine.

The technical progress involved here is recognised by the workers who use the machines. When one was installed at the Michell Bearing plant, groups of men were always to be found watching the details of the installation, talking with the German technicians, marvelling at the size of the table. In the nearby Vickers' Crabtree factory in Gateshead a shop steward noted that,

> In the first instance these machines came as a bit of a challenge. Operating all machinery can be very monotonous and when you get something new it livens your day. It eventually becomes monotonous but at the beginning it is challenging especially learning to set it up. Apprentices are dying to get on to it . . .

At the Scotswood works, where they were anticipating the NC lathe one shop steward described the feelings of his members,

> For the skilled man, what he'll be interested in is seeing what type of machine it is, how it's working and how it's going to affect him. It will be like a new toy to him at first . . . I don't think in this modern day and age people hit back as individuals and say 'that's done away with my skills, all I do now is push the button instead of working it right out' . . . But it definitely does take the skills off that job.

Here is one part of the problem of technical change. The NC machines themselves do not dictate that the worker, the person who operates them, couldn't 'work it right out'. There is no *technical* reason why the NC lathe operator shouldn't also be the programmer and the technician. After all, the knowledge of practical engineering required for programming is already mastered by the skilled machinist. The process of programming on the basis of a design – drawn up as before by a draughtsman – is essentially the same work as when the machinist took the drawing to the shop floor; there is only the additional skill of programming to be learnt.

That such a possibility seems unlikely makes clear that these changes, like the rationalisation we discussed earlier, are not neutral ones. NC machines are introduced on the factory floors by management. To them they represent extremely expensive units of capital investment which must secure a return; and this return can best be guaranteed by reducing the size of the labour force and controlling its activities. Mike Cooley of the Lucas Aerospace combine committee has noted some of the likely consequences of this:

> Confronted with equipment which is getting obsolete literally by the minute, and has involved enormous capital investment the employer will seek to recoup his investment by exploiting the equipment for 24 hours per day. In consequence the employer will seek to eliminate so-called non-productive time, such as tea breaks, will seek to subordinate the operators more and more to the machine in order to get the maximum performance, and will insist either that the equipment is worked on three shifts to obtain 24-hour exploitation, or is used on a continuous overtime basis.[4]

As yet Vickers owns but a few NC machines, and these have not been in operation long enough for a new division of labour to have become established. But all the indications are that it will develop in this way – unless workers organise to alter the process. Certainly Lord Robens has a clear picture of what an automated Vickers will mean for those who work there:

> In this industry we are pushing more and more highly qualified technicians into the back rooms. We will require more and more of these people – people who would have been craftsmen – in the design rooms and the jobs on the shop floor itself will be pushing buttons. This is where the slow starters or those who still don't make it will be employed.

While the question of deskilling and a new division of labour within engineering factories is an important one, the most pressing manifestation of this change for workers at Vickers is the related question of 'job loss' and unemployment. To quote Lord Robens again, understandably, they are also worried about their jobs and the effects of these machines on their security . . . we realise this and that is why we try to plan the way in which we introduce the machines. We try to plan things in a way which allows us to introduce the machines without disrupting the workplace, making people redundant and so on.

'Natural wastage' depletes the workforce; NC machines take up the slack. Because of the gradual way in which NC machines are being introduced, stewards are only just recognising the massive problems of the future. A shop steward at South Marston is clear about this: 'We've all gone wrong on the introduction of semi-automated processes. I'm sure it will cut the workforce by a third or more. No union has produced any guidelines to shop stewards to deal with the problem.'

This is a point echoed by shop stewards at Vickers' Crabtree factory in Gateshead:

The danger with numerically-controlled machines is that the shop stewards do not realise the danger until it's too late to get anything done about it. By that time they've done away with five men, the two who ended up working the machines are quite happy with the little bit of extra money they're getting: so you can't go back. You've got to have foresight, you've got to know the consequences of management's action. In the capstan section where they've introduced two automatic capstans it's just about halved the section through 'natural wastage' and it's reduced overtime.

The trends – and the dilemmas – involved here are crucial ones. In the early 1970s in the USA the giant machine tool company Cincinnati Milacron of Ohio commissioned a report from the International Institution for Production Engineering Research. The report examined the likely penetration and utilisation of computer controlled product systems within manufacturing industry. The institute concluded that:

1 By 1980 a computer software system for full automation and optimisation of all steps in the manufacture of a part will be developed and in wide use.

2 By 1985 full on-line automation and optimisation of complete
   manufacturing plants controlled by a central computer will be
   a reality.
3 By 1990 more than 50 per cent of the machine tools
   produced will not have a 'stand alone' use, but will be part
   of a versatile manufacturing system, featuring automatic
   part handling between stations, and being controlled from a
   central process computer.

Furthermore the researchers felt that on the basis of their
discussions,

> Overall it can be seen that there is a very strong consensus
> that the coming of the computer-automated factory will in
> general have no harmful economic, social or environmental
> effects, but that there is some significant doubt as to whether
> this is wholly true for the factory workers.[5]

An awareness of the possible dimension of the 'problems for factory
workers' has only recently been considered in Britain (the main
problem here has been seen as a lack of the right sort of investment).
However, encouraged by the government and the machine tool
manufacturers own talk of 'reduced direct operator costs and no
more problems on the shop floor', British industrialists have begun
to invest in automated and semi-automated processes. It was in this
context that Ken Corfield, the managing director of Standard
Telephones and Cables, addressed the 1977 annual meeting of the
Royal Society. His speech was reported extensively in the *Financial
Times*:

> Mr Corfield demonstrated how different the new production
> lines would be from the large 'metal bashing' factories that used
> to make electro-mechanical switching. The new lines would be
> laboratory-like, producing electronics as a continuous and
> automatic process, virtually untouched by hand.
>   Moreover, he forecast that over the next ten years the
> 'capability' of each cubic inch of electronics would increase a
> further thousand-fold. 'The impact on our people will be
> dramatic and, as is usually the case, it will probably be with
> us physically before we have made the necessary
> psychological and philosophical adjustments.'

Jobs vanish a new 'industry' moves in

A MAJOR chunk of industrial Newcastle has turned into a gh_ area for jobs.

An investigation has revealed that the spread of vast warehous_ on the once-bustling Scotswood Road has sounded the employment dea_ knell for thousands of workers.

On one site, where Vickers tractor division once employed mor_ than 1,000, only 87 people work in two massive warehouses which straddle the land between the Tyne and Scotswood Road.

'The joke about a semiconductor company becoming so successful that it had to move into smaller premises is, in reality, a social comment the implications of which have gone largely unheeded at Westminster and Transport House.

'Few ministers, for example, seem to have grasped the implications for industry to invest. Industrial investment, whether in revamped or entirely new factories, is largely synonymous with what once was known as automation. The pressures on industry to minimise its use of people are immense.'

Increased investment is essential if British companies are to survive but investment by no means guarantees new jobs. The evidence of recent years is quite the reverse. For many people this appears as a total and inescapable contradiction. For example the South Marston shop steward who earlier pointed to the importance of job loss also says,

> You just have to have these machines. In a capitalist society, as I said before, you have to have the equipment if you're going to compete. Some of the machines they have in there: I think York museum would pay a fortune for them. But its how they go about it. Some of those automated production lines that I've seen a film of can do 27 operations including hardening and tempering. And nobody touched it. Its a bit frightening really.

It *is* a bit frightening. In engineering and allied industries between 1963 and 1973 there has been a 33.5 per cent increase in plant and machinery at constant replacement cost, but at the same time there has been an 11.9 per cent decrease in jobs. To quote once again from Dan Sharpe's article, 'gone are the days when it would be said that profits create employment'. The ASTMS research department has estimated that increased investment in heavy engineering will see the silicone chip microprocessor replacing 200,000 of the 475,000 jobs in the industry by 1995. On the basis of estimates offered by firms in 21 leading industries the research team calculate a job loss (in those industries alone) of almost 2 million during the same period. On these estimates unemployment totals of over 5 million in the 1990s seem likely.[6]

Property values

In examining the paradox of Vickers' transformation into a 'modern corporation' we have, up until now, directed attention to the changes which have taken place *within* the factories. This is just one side of the story, however. To complete the picture we need to remember that it is 'finance' which is at the back of all these changes. Vickers Ltd. was forced to change as a result of a crisis of profitability. Take-overs, rationalisation and a certain degree of restructuring have averted that crisis. A further paradox of this development lies in the extent to which Vickers, in the search for greater profit, has shifted away from industrial production altogether. This has involved the development of Vickers' property interests.

In June 1975, *Vickers News* reported on 'The positive attitude of the company in creating new prospects for industrial expansion at Swindon [which] was emphasised by Vickers' managing director, Sir Peter Matthews, when he officially opened the first phase of the South Marston Industrial Estate.'

However most of that expansion – at South Marston and in the Swindon area generally – has taken the form of warehousing. The extent of this priority of 'property values' over production and employment is seen most dramatically on Tyneside. There most of the site of the old Scotswood works has also been turned over to warehousing. The 1973 *Annual Report* noted that this site is suitable for 'industrial development'. In order to carry out this development Vickers collaborated with Drum Developments, a Dublin property company with considerable experience in the north east. They formed a joint subsidiary company of Vickers called Inter-Vickers Ltd. In 1973 Inter-Vickers applied for planning permission to erect light industrial/warehouse units on the whole of the site. But because warehousing provides so few jobs the Newcastle council gave planning permission for only about half the site. The city planning office in a letter to the works convenor at Scotswood put their approach like this: 'In order to monitor the situation it was agreed that no planning permission would be given for phase 2 until evidence could be shown that phase 1 was making sufficient progress towards achieving an overall employment total for the Scotswood site.'

As a result the council's Industrial Development Committee turned down Vickers' application. However, they informed the company that if the application was amended to 'light industrial purposes only' it would receive favourable treatment. By September 1975 over half of phase 1 had been leased to Boots the Chemist, and the application stated that this would provide 'possible employment for about 60 people' a relatively high ratio for non-industrial use. Further the council was told that Vickers had received no applications for the industrial use of the site and they had no such

---

Companies making forklift trucks have serious difficulties in keeping pace with their foreign competitors because present users of many vehicles are changing to automated warehousing systems with mixtures of driverless trucks and other methods for moving materials.

Large retail distribution chains require a new warehouse every six to seven years. The next generation of warehouses built for such customers will be fully automated, requiring a tenth of the labour. Thus employment in the large retailing sector is liable to grow more slowly than turnover.

The Times, 17 July 1978

---

plans themselves. Without planning permission, the inference ran, the site would remain underdeveloped and Newcastle would suffer an absolute loss of jobs and rates. In the end the council compromised and granted permission for warehouses to be built on 50 per cent of the second site so long as the rest was restricted to industrial uses. Optimistically they argued that: 'the situation is not black and white, since it is possible that a warehousing firm moving to the site would release buildings elsewhere for industrial use at a relatively low cost.'

This, however, proved unfounded. At a time when there should have been 60 workers on the Boots site, a survey conducted by the Benwell Community Development Project found only nine.[7] Furthermore only 87 of the 400 jobs which the 1976 report anticipated would be provided by Boots and N.E. Distributors (who moved to the site from a cramped city centre building) have been created so far. No industrial tenants have been found for the second part of phase 2.

The point here is not that Vickers is going out of its way to be anti-social, to attract low-employment activities like warehousing rather than industry. After all, the rent that each would pay would be the same. The point is that Vickers seems to have no special preference for what sort of activity goes on along the Scotswood Road, so long as it gets the rent without undue delay. The interests of Vickers Properties are met by responding to market forces. In the last few years – and in the foreseeable future – the big retailing concerns have demanded warehousing; and they pay the rent. That this market pressure does not coincide with the needs of the people who live and want to work in and around West Newcastle is – according to this logic – of little consequence. A useful book called *The Property Machine* sums it up: 'The property system does not look upon property as an asset in a social and environmental sense. Property is a financial asset and the location and character of development are determined by investment criteria.'[8]

This is the nature of 'modernisation' generally. This is the force which has produced the development of the 'new Vickers'. It is the dominance of accounting logic which has produced Vickers in this way. As Ford includes the benefits and costs of burn deaths and injuries in its arithmetic calculations, so do companies like Vickers shift and move, close down and alter. But the 'hidden costs' are there to be seen and experienced. They are high enough for people to want to 'do something about it' and to ask whether there cannot be an alternative and better ways.

Part 3

THE WORKERS' RESPONSE – COMBINE!

Parts one and two of this report have attempted to convey an impression of the power which Vickers – like other giant corporations – has at its disposal. But it would be wrong to imagine that this power is unchallengeable. While capital is much more flexible today than it was even twenty years ago, it is not *completely* flexible. It has to establish factories somewhere and it has to employ workers to work in them to create the profits. Workers can turn this indispensability to their advantage by organisation.

Trade union organisations developed historically in response to a particular problem and to a particular kind of capitalism. A craft union like the Amalgamated Society of Engineers developed to defend the interests of skilled men. Its geographically-based (as opposed to factory-based) branches and quasi-autonomous districts reflected the movement of craftsmen between particular factories and also the local ownership of those factories. The first shop steward 'combines', which developed in response to 'dilution' (i.e. downgrading of skill levels) around the time of the first world war, reflected this need for *local* liaison between shop steward committees. In places like the Clyde and Sheffield these organisations allowed people working in different factories for different employers to discuss and organise around a common experience. A geo- graphically-based structure has always been an important source of strength to the engineering unions. Arguably, given the increasing centralisation of control within the giant corporations, such a structure can now be seen as the source of some problems.

No matter how separate and autonomous one plant may appear during the normal day-to-day course of events, in times of crisis the essential interdependence of the whole of the corporation's operations is more clear. And at those times it is clear that purely plant-based organisation is not enough. Action at regional level, through the respective district committee of the union, can be effective, but that too, in itself, is an inadequate basis for a challenge to the power of the big corporation.

In the 1950s shop stewards in multi-plant corporations began to extend their organisation beyond their own particular factory and the official union organisation. They set up a form of shop steward committee which was known as the *combine* committee. Les Gurl of the British Leyland Combine Committee explained how stewards in the old BMC group came to extend their contacts beyond the plant:

> During the past 25 years vast changes have taken place, followed by closures of factories and the dismissal of the workers who worked in those factories. When mergers take place the top management would meet to discuss re-organisation, it was therefore important that workers and union members had a committee where stewards could meet, sometimes at very short notice, to look at problems covering the whole group, thus the BMC Joint Shop Stewards Committee.

It has become clear to many of Vickers' workers that, as a consequence of all the costs and problems outlined in part two, some form of company-wide organisation of trade unionists is essential. The task of building such an organisation is a difficult one however, and the aim of this part of the *Workers' Report* is to make clear both the strengths and weaknesses of the movement toward combine committees, at Vickers and elsewhere.

Chapter 9

'Why Should They Want to Meet?'

The experience of stewards in Vickers has been similar to that at BMC. It has led some of them to see the need for a committee which directly links all sections of the company's workforce and is based upon the established plant committees. Critics of the combine committee, however, will argue that as yet only a minority of the company's plants are actively involved in the committee's work. Some will go on to say that this is an indication of its lack of relevance. As one of the company's personnel officers put it: 'Why should they want to meet? What have people who make printing equipment in common with people who make tanks?' In many ways this is a good question. The answer, however, is not as simple as this man implies. Certainly, discussions with shop steward committees within Vickers (both those involved in the combine committee and those who are not) reveals that people have thought about the problems. It also reveals an attitude which is broadly in sympathy with the aims of combine organisation: a feeling that this (for all the difficulties) provides the only basis for dealing with the problems posed by a company such as Vickers. Here is how a convenor at one of the plants which has been involved in the combine committee from the beginning sees the situation:

> The combine committee is a very important development. It is the means of establishing the basis for eventual negotiations with head office about all major issues. It could have the ability to gather a wide range of facts from the various plants which could be invaluable in negotiations. But it will have to be highly organised to combat the policy decisions of multinational companies.
>
> A common problem faced by trade unionists are the

traditional jealousies that exist between groups of workers.
Jealousies that have existed for years. The main issue is that
groups like Vickers can exploit this – particularly when
redundancy situations arise. That's why we *need* to develop an
organisation which can cut across these lines. Also a committee is
essential to establish common benefits for workers in all
Vickers' plants. We need to exchange information on patterns
and trends within the group. We *must* be forewarned if we
are ever going to combat redundancy.

Representatives from committees who have only recently joined
the combine say similar things:

I believe firmly that combine committees are the only way
forward when up against multinational companies such as
Vickers who seem to change their management as often as
one changes clothes. We joined the combine soon after the
take-over and the information which the combine has
provided has been very helpful.

Here's another account:

The combine committee first made an impact at the national
pension meeting. Our representatives there noticed that there
was a group talking as one, and that they seemed to be the
only people from the shop floor who knew what was going
on. So we decided to join and since then the information has
been great – that has been the main thing. Before we joined
the combine we didn't even know what companies were
involved in Vickers.

And another

In negotiations I frequently quote the rate throughout the
combine. They don't like you knowing – and it certainly works
in bargaining with them. We would not have got bereavement
leave, time off for hospital appointments and dental
appointments if we didn't get the information from the
combine. There was never any opposition to it. We started a
shop fund as soon as we got involved. Everyone paid up – we
all knew it was for the combine.

Several plant committees have experienced some disagreement over the value of the committee: they tell of arguments over the value of the £5 affiliation fee and the cost of sending delegates to the quarterly meetings. But in spite of the arguments people realise that the presence of a combine committee still exerts an influence:

> Some of the stewards say they have little time for the combine – they don't want to serve as a delegate to Leeds (they'll lose their Saturday overtime!). But they use all the information that comes from the combine. It's all used one way or another. And if they're honest they'd admit that they couldn't do their job as a steward in this plant properly without the information that the combine provides.

In a multi-plant firm, operating a wide range of production systems and paying an equally wide range of wage rates and fringe benefits, *information* is something for which all shop stewards feel the need. Providing this information has been an essential function of the combine committee and something which *all* affiliated committees claim to have benefited from. But the aims of the committee do not stop there and its members (even its least active ones) imagine a wider role for it in the future. Here are the views of a shop steward in one of the company's smaller and more isolated plants:

> I'd like to see it develop as one body. If there's a dispute in one factory the whole lot do their utmost to support that dispute. If one factory comes out – the whole lot comes out! That's the way we should be going.

And another in the engineering group:

> I can see the combine committee becoming a really effective body. Nowadays, investment plans, production plans, wages and conditions throughout the whole combine – these are the important things. And the combine committee must emerge as the body to carry out these negotiations.

Often the expectations are so strong (and the need felt so urgently) that they surface as doubts and criticisms of 'the way the combine is going'. People 'wonder if we will really make it in this company', and in several of the affiliated plants the issue of the combine's development has emerged as a source of conflict at times. A shop steward in one such plant put his views in this way:

> The combine should be organised within the Vickers structures to fight all injustices within the company. It *could* and *should* utilise all the information it receives for a collective attack on these injustices. Universal action to obtain for all workers at Vickers wages and conditions compatible with the top 50 per cent of Vickers workers today. We must get negotiating rights! These are the things the combine should be doing. We should be going beyond *information* and getting some action.

Before we turn to the problems involved in organising this action and to a detailed examination of the combine committee we should pay some attention to the shop stewards committees which are not affiliated to the combine. Here too – in all but two of the plants – there is a general agreement with, and sympathy toward, the aims of the combine committee. A steward from one of the Roneo Vickers plants put it like this

> Although Roneo Vickers is just one part of the Vickers group we know that all the money goes into one big kitty – Millbank Tower. Basically we're all working for the same governor. It's because of this that I like the idea of a combine. All being in together sort of thing. The main problem for us is the expense of getting to Leeds and of convincing people that its worth putting a few coins in to send somebody up.

This response is a common one. Shop steward committees note that they 'weren't aware' of the combine's activities, or that while agreeing with the aims of combine committee organisation, their own domestic organisation wasn't strong enough to carry further, external involvement. Others – particularly shop stewards in the smaller isolated plants – felt that they had very little to contribute:

> Links could be very useful for us I suppose. I don't know if the other plants of Vickers would get much out of links with us though. It could be interesting for them I suppose – it would certainly give them a hell of a lot to laugh at!

This leaves the two plants – one of them amongst the highest paid in the company – whose shop steward committees felt that involvement in the combine would not serve their interests. On the contrary, they felt that combine-wide negotiations may lead them to lose their established wage differentials:

> I suppose the committee felt that we had a choice between concerning ourselves with the interests of our own members or getting involved with 'brotherhood'. We're only brothers to a certain extent you see. If we're all going to share and share alike, the lions will start roaring if they have to share with the pussycats.

Here, the committee's decision had been reinforced by management's advice:

> Whatever you do, don't reveal this in Leeds. If this (agreement) becomes common knowledge you'll just end up tying our hands in this plant.

At the other plant the local union official had been given the same advice. In both of these committees however there is talk of 'the more long term view'. Some shop stewards argue the need for seeing the interests of their members beyond the present wage packet:

> We need to convince the membership that we cannot carry on by simply following our short term interests. In this day and age we're going to have to look a long way ahead. We've seen the consequences of some of these new processes in this plant already. We've got to get away from looking over our shoulder at the other fella. If other factories drag themselves up that's a good thing. We have nothing to lose. We'll gain because we'll be able to make advances together.

To date, though, this has been a minority view in this plant.

Clearly there has been a lot of discussion of the combine committee within Vickers Ltd. over the last year or so. In the plants, at union meetings and at Millbank Tower the prospects of the committee have been weighed up and argued over. Occasionally, the discussion has been heated. The emergence of the combine committee touches upon issues of real importance, and it is important now that this report stands back a bit and looks at the development and future prospects of the committee within Vickers.

Mr E. Goodinson,   Jany14th   9
8 Ordnance Place
Sheffield.

Dear Sir and Brother,

            I have been instructed by the Shop Stewards
of the above firm to apply for affilliation to the Combine and
therefore I request that you furnish us with full particulars,
how many delegates are we allowed? the affilliation fees on
4,000 workers, date of next meeting etc.

            Should our application be accepted our
delegate to the first meeting will be the Works Convenor.
Hoping to hear from you soon, with best wishes.

                        Yours fraternally,

            Coun

                        Works Convenor.

Vickers' Combine Shop Stewards Committee

Secretary's Address

E. GOODINSON,
8 ORDNANCE PLACE,
SHEFFIELD, 9.

Your Reference...... 7. 2. 1949

Dear Bro Bradley.

Sorry for the delay,
but the meeting is fixed for
11AM Sunday Feb 13/49 at the
"Crown Hotel" which is at the
corner of Fountain St and Booth St
Manchester, Booth St faces the
entrance to Manchester Art Gallery
Mosely St.

Hoping to see you there
Yours fraternally
E Goodinson

NB In all probability I shall look
the place up on Saturday night

Chapter 10

The Making of the Combine Committee

The Beginnings of a national committee

Since the war there have been several attempts by local shop stewards' organisations to establish contact with stewards in other Vickers plants. Usually such contact was made first on a regional basis: for example contact between Scotswood and Elswick on Tyneside[1], and in Wiltshire between the South Marston stewards and other of the company's aircraft plants in the area. Occasionally attempts were made to extend these regional links. A steward at South Marston remembers how, in the 1950s, they tried to move out from the 'aircraft combine': 'We tried, we tried a few times. But Barrow was always the stumbling block. They didn't seem to want to know about anybody else.' In the north east the main contact outside the area was with Sheffield and the union representative in the Vickers' steel plants: 'Sheffield was always the place. In the 1950s the convenors were often down there. Mainly on questions to do with the rate of pay, but that was the basis of the combine in the 1950s.'

These early attempts to build a shop stewards' organisation that extended beyond the plant and the locality were frustrated by the rationalisation, run down, take-over and nationalisation which altered the company in the 1960s. Steel nationalisation took the Sheffield works out of Vickers, and the formation of BAC effectively isolated another group of workers. Throughout this period rank-and-file trade unionists have had to adjust and re-adjust their vision of the corporation. As contacts have been lost new ones have had to be sought, as one network lost its significance others have had to be woven. Always a process of adjustment to the reality of corporate and state decision-making.

This was the context within which the people who worked in

Vickers' plants, began to think about establishing an organisation capable of responding more adequately to the problems they were facing in the company. It led them to set up, in November 1974, the national shop stewards combine committee: the first committee at Vickers to consolidate informal contacts into regular national meetings; to back those meetings with a secretary and the formal exchange of information; and to have the further aim of making united approaches to Vickers House.

The impetus for this committee has been located within the 'old Vickers'. Most of these plants had faced similar difficulties during the restructuring of the corporation. To quote one steward from the South Marston plant:

> Since 1969, Vickers' policy had been clear for everyone to see: it's to divide, to isolate, to breakdown, to have a look at, and to cut off if it's not profitable, and to invest if it is.
> That's why we needed a combine and these are the important things (as well as wages and conditions) for the combine to deal with.

Throughout these years the shop stewards in the old Vickers plants had been in contact with each other. An early activist from the north east describes how:

> We had a lot of contact with other plants over the movement of work, in order to find out the piece prices at the plants where the work came from; and we had seen the experiences of other combines; it seemed obvious that we needed one of our own in Vickers.

At the various plants of Crabtree Vickers in Leeds, managements' moves to integrate production had brought the shop stewards into closer contact. This was reinforced at Water Lane where the fight to control the movement of work and of men had also revealed the need to organise beyond the printing machinery plants. In that plant, management's attempt to sub-contract work out of the company prompted the feeling that a combine organisation was becoming a necessity:

> There is an inbred dislike of sub-contracting so we were always objecting to it. And eventually the company, in response to our objections and to spare capacity at

Report on wages in the Vickers groups

The following establishments in the Vickers Group are the collated reports received up to July 1977.

CRABTREE GATESHEAD. Skilled (piecework) £51.80 to £73.50. Semi skilled (piecework) £51.80 to £52.50. Labourer (based on factory average) £47.50 to £50.00.

CRABTREE OTLEY. Fitters average (directs) £66.36., (indirects) £61.05. Skilled Machinists average (directs) £67.20, (indirects) £61.05. Semi-skilled £53.90. Labourers £50.15.

LEEDS WATER LANE. Skilled average (piecework) £62.00. Skilled (indirect) £63.00. Semi skilled average (piecework) £54.00 to £56.00. Labourer lowest grade £52.00.

KEARNY TRECKER MARWIN BRIGHTON. Fitters £51.55 to £62.05. Skilled machinists £49.45 to £58.90. Crane Drivers £47.65 to £50.46. Labourers £44.28 to £46.38.

SCOTSWOOD NEWCASTLE. Skilled £57.25 to £59.00. Semi skilled £49.65 to £54.10. Labourers £44.70 to £47.70. All rates plus 5% with minimum £2.50.

KIRKBYMOORSIDE. Skilled £55.65 to £61.00. Semi skilled £53.55. Polisher £71.50 Brakepress operator £65.00.

SOUTH MARSTON SWINDON. Toolmakers £55.00. Fitters £54.00. Skilled machinists £54.00. All rates plus 5% semi skilled £48.15. plus £2.50.

MICHELLS NEWCASTLE. Skilled £64.52. Skilled machinists £60.32. Semi-skilled £58.75. Ancillarys £54.02. Labourers £52.45.

THETFORD VICKERS DAWSON. Skilled average £64.00. Semi skilled £59.00. to £62.00. Labourers £52.00.

ELSWICK NEWCASTLE. Skilled average (piecework) £71.27. Machinists average £64.35. Ancillary workers £56.24 to £62.76. Craneman and Slingers £59.95. Time served indirects (inspectors maintainance) receive skilled average.

The following Vickers establishments have not submitted wage reports, Barrow in Furness, Brown Bro's, Crayford, Dartford, Rhayader, Vickers Dawson Gomersal, Crabtree Hunslet, Howson Algraphy Batley, Crabtree Foundry Otley.

Scotswood, wanted to shift work to Scotswood. The combine would have been very useful in this situation. On another occasion they wanted to bring fitters from Scotswood to Water Lane for a short-time. We agreed to this. But we had no links with stewards at Scotswood. It would have been very beneficial to have been able to sort this problem out at combine level.

These changes within Vickers were also affected by the actions of trade unionists in other companies. Combine committees spread during the 1960s and these developments were discussed in the Vickers plants and also at meetings of the Institute for Workers Control which were attended by several of the Vickers shop stewards. In this way – through a combination of 'internal' and 'external' factors – the Vickers Shop Stewards National Combine Committee was set up. Based on the old Vickers it aimed to combat the policies of the new Vickers. *Shop Floor Voice*, the combine committee's newspaper, describes the process in this way:

In the autumn of 1974 at a meeting in the Leeds Trades Club the Vickers' Shop Stewards National Combine Committee was launched. For some time it had been apparent to the advanced shop stewards committees that their local managements were on some issues ventriloquists' dummies mouthing the dictates of Vickers House. Given this situation it was necessary to match the Vickers' management organisation on a national and international basis by at least a national organisation on the part of trade union members in the group.

Since that first meeting, the combine committee has met on a regular, quarterly, basis in Leeds. The delegates arrive late on Friday afternoon and normally stay at the Hotel Metropole. It's rather posh and a bit expensive but it has a lot of space, and a late bar. Friday evening is spent talking and drinking. Peter Tolchard organises the taxis; clubs are visited and beer drunk. Delegates from the south worry that they can't understand the Geordie dialect. In between all this they thrash out the details of the last three months: the changes in wage rates, manning levels and management tactics since they last met. Discussion and argument carry through until the early hours. The Hotel Metropole provides a kettle in each room with coffee and biscuits: you're glad of that when you wake in the morning to prepare for the formal business at the Trades and Labour Club. This business covers a variety of issues, the central one being detailed reports on the situation at each of the plants represented at the meeting. Usually there are no surprises. The purpose of the meeting is to establish the continuity of the combine organisation and to solidify (through formal commitments and agreement) the telephone contacts, letters and informal chat that has gone on before. Above all else the Leeds' meetings establish the reality of the combine committee. These meetings make it clear (to management, shop steward committees and union officials) that the combine committee will not just go away; they establish the fact that the combine committee functions as an effective organisation and that it has to be treated as something permanent.

Parity

From the beginning the shop stewards involved in the combine committee have been concerned with the wages and fringe benefits provided by their employer. To quote again from *Shop Floor Voice*:

> Our first task as a combine was to get a picture of the wages and conditions in the group and some of the information was quite startling. Wide differences of up to £20 per week in some cases were being paid to people doing identical jobs, and also conditions had been introduced in some factories that were not applying in others.

The first practical step taken by the combine committee was to establish the extent of anomalies throughout the company. Questionnaires requesting information on the level of wages and fringe benefits were sent to each affiliated committee, who then received from the secretary a detailed report of rates and conditions throughout the company. In 1978 this report became incorporated into the combine's quarterly newspaper *Shop Floor Voice* (see insert). Every shop stewards committee found this information useful. In the words of one steward from Leeds:

> The parity question is something which management feel a bit vulnerable to. They don't like you knowing what people

are getting in other plants. Often they don't know themselves!
I quoted something to one of our personnel managers about
Thetford and he said 'Thetford, where's that?' He didn't
know Vickers had a plant there.

The parity argument *is* a strong one. Information on wage rates
throughout the company can provide a strong basis for breaking
much of the 'divide and rule' tactics which can be operated by a
company like Vickers. Frequently shop stewards have been able to
utilise the information contained in the wages report to good
purpose. A steward from Thetford notes how: 'it was the easiest
negotiation I've ever had. I just told them what the other rates were
and they just gave it us. Just like that.'

The need for this kind of information is one of the basic reasons
for joining the national combine committee:

We've come up against the argument time after time in
negotiations: 'It's Vickers policy that you will only get this.'
Time after time we've heard it 'this is the policy for the
Vickers group'. And we didn't know if it was or if it wasn't
like. So we explained to the members – by joining the
combine we could find out the evidence. We could go into
negotiations with stronger arguments. And in the end it was a
winner. They voted us down on one meeting but three
months later they voted unanimously for us to go to Leeds –
and made the biggest collection that we've ever had off the
shop floor.

The collection and use of information has not been limited to wage
rates alone. While Millbank Tower (the banker) exerts a centralised
control over the company's investment plan, the responsibility for
the treatment of the men and women who turn that investment into
profit is largely decentralised. So as wage rates vary, so too do other
aspects of the workers' employment situation. In some plants the
company supplied safety shoes, a facility which was laughed out of
court in others. So too with overalls, safety spectacles and the like.
Neither did the company provide uniform welfare facilities (e.g.
bereavement leave) or sickness schemes. Payment while off work
through illness varied from plant to plant. (In most cases the
payment was near the derisory level of four pounds.)

The combine committee organisation through the distribution of information and (in the case of sickness payments) through the recommendation that there be a concerted effort in all plant negotiations, has also achieved a levelling up of fringe benefits paid by the company. The principle followed in all cases has been to press for the levelling up of all plants to the standard achieved in the best. The fears of some of the high wage plants that a levelling down process would operate thus seem exaggerated. Perhaps the example of sickness pay illustrates this best. The combine committee took a decision in 1977 to recommend that all affiliated plants make the demand for a substantial increase in sickness pay one of their priorities in the 1977–78 pay round. All plants followed this recommendation and as each plant settled the terms were communicated to the others. South Marston achieved the £20 breakthrough in January, and this news was received with a surprise that verged on disbelief in some plants. At Leeds a shop steward remembers how:

> Well we couldn't believe it at first. We had meetings with the members on the sections and we were all really surprised by it. I know our management were. They made it clear that we weren't going to get what South Marston got. We accepted that. But when one plant has got a £16 increase it makes it easier to ask for £7. It certainly made our negotiations a lot easier. There's no doubt about that.

Of course all this – the use of information in bargaining, the pursuit of wage parity etc. – is standard trade union practice. On all these issues – wage rates, sickness schemes, safety – the presence of the combine committee has exerted an important influence upon the balance of power in plant negotiations. The information link-up provided by the committee has proven to be an essential adjunct to the plant committee in its orthodox activity of bargaining over wage rates with the employer. In this respect the combine committee has filled a gap that existed between shop floor organisation and the full-time official union structures. This point is worth stressing (and we will return to it later): the growth of multi-plant organisations within the corporate sector of the economy has made clear the need for a new kind of trade union organisation. The thrust for this development has not come from the official union structures but rather from below – from the shop floor committees that have been forced to deal with the new situation.

The organisation of solidarity

The collection of information on wage rates and the like has been but one aspect of the making of the Vickers combine committee. The formalised link-ups between the plants has also proved useful in cases where individual plants have been involved in industrial disputes. As individual shop steward committees gain information on wages so too do they learn of other issues. 'Information' is obtained through social contact (through telephone calls and letters), a contact which is strengthened every three months or so at Leeds. In this way the various shop steward committees learn of the experiences of workers and shop stewards in other plants and come to a better understanding of the kinds of problems experienced throughout the company. Such an understanding is important in times of crisis: when 'acts of solidarity' – the blacking of work, the provision of moral and financial support and, occasionally, sympathetic strike action – may be needed from other plants. Such issues also serve to make clear the *interdependence* of workers who are employed by a company like Vickers.

The *potential* for this kind of contact and support was clearly seen by the shop stewards and workers at Water Lane at the time of the plant closure: an organised combine committee would have made a lot of difference at that time. Lately (and particularly in the north east) workers in particular plants *have* been able to benefit from their organised links with workers in other Vickers' plants. In 1976 the workers at Vickers Crabtree plant in Gateshead experienced the same forces that had been brought to bear on the Water Lane plant. In the words of a shop steward: 'we used to be tied in with Water Lane but when that was cut we were on our own as a sub-division of Crabtree. Profit accounting was established on a plant-by-plant basis, and of course that meant that management began to push.'

As part of the push at Gateshead, management proposed an adjustment to the bonus payment scheme which in effect amounted to a wage cut. After protracted negotiations a mass meeting voted for a strike which was to last eight weeks. During the strike the shop stewards committee at Gateshead obtained through the regional links established within the combine framework the full support of the workers in the other plants on the Tyne, and the blacking of all work for the Gateshead factory throughout the company. No work for the plant left the Elswick foundry and machines for the factory remained untouched at Water Lane – something which held up work throughout the printing machinery division. Collections were made on Tyneside, and throughout the other Crabtree plants. This support culminated in a meeting of all the shop stewards from the Vickers plants on Tyneside. This joint shop stewards meeting affirmed 'full moral and financial support' for the strike, guaranteed the continuation of the blacking and raised the suggestion of the extension of the strike along the Tyne. The convenor of the Crabtree plant is in no doubt as to the effect of these actions upon the course of the dispute:

> 'Unity' that's what it's all about really. Our strike showed just what could be achieved. There's no doubt in my mind that the settlement we obtained – the increase in wages instead of the back-dated reduction that the company was trying to impose – was due to the unity that was shown by the plants on Tyneside. The support that came from that meeting in the St. Stevens Church Hall on the Scotswood Road (the very fact that that meeting took place) made it clear to the company and to the members in Crabtrees that we weren't fighting alone. And that's the main thing: we have to get it across to the members that support *will* be forthcoming in major disputes; that if you work in a factory for Vickers, you're not just by yourself.

A victory then; and lots of lessons learned. There was more than money won in this strike. The strike (and the solidarity that supported it) greatly strengthened the shop floor organisation at Gateshead. The stewards say that:

> Things have changed enormously since the strike. It really established the shop steward committee in this plant. We've established the right to have meetings during the company's time. We've got a lot more respect from the blokes and we can rely on their support now. When a steward was sacked recently we immediately got him reinstated.

The relationship between the plant-based shop stewards committees and the combine is not one-way, therefore. The presence of the combine can support the development of the individual committees (and vice versa). As with wage rates the combine organisation can facilitate the 'levelling up' of the organised shop floor strength of workers within Vickers. This was seen clearly by one of the early 'combine activists' in Leeds.

> A strong shop floor organisation is a necessary prerequisite for a strong combine committee, which is itself an essential element of factory organisation if we are going to be able to counter management. The two *must* go ahead together.

A further illustration of this interdependence is provided by the experience of the workers at the Scotswood plant on Tyneside. This plant (as we have seen in chapter three) was threatened with heavy redundancies in 1977. The linkage with the combine organisation gave an added impetus to the shop stewards committee in their decision to refuse to accept any further run-down. The confidence they gained from this successful struggle, carried over into the annual pay negotiations in the autumn. In this the shop stewards committee was determined that Scotswood was not to be kept open as a low wage plant, that 'jobs' had to mean 'jobs that paid the going rate'.

Vickers has traditionally paid among the highest rates for skilled engineering workers on the Tyne, and in the post-war period the piece rates at Scotswood were just above the rate at Elswick. During the 1970s (and the period of run-down) this changed and the workers at Scotswood were particularly badly hit. There were a number of reasons for this, the principal one being that in 1973 the Scotswood management (in an attempt to regulate wage payments) had replaced piece-rate payments with a form of measured day work. In effect this meant that the Scotswood workers were paid on a fixed hourly rate but with an added production bonus. As a consequence of this change, the Labour Government's wage controls, and the vulnerability of the plant, the wages of the Scotswood workers fell steadily behind those paid at Elswick (still on piece rates) and the other engineering plants in the area. This fact (supported by the wage report from the combine) convinced the workers at Scotswood, that the time had come for them to do something about it.

We were clear about it from the outset, like. We know the
kind of wages being paid in this area – for skilled factory
work, you know. And this management just isn't paying the
rate. We used to be the best paid plant in the area – now
we're well down the list. At Elswick they're taking home £7 a
week more than we are. And it's the same in other parts of
the company. £55 a week is not a good rate for a skilled man.

They were clear from the outset that Vickers 'had better come up
with something this time'. When the company didn't, when
management refused to take the negotiations seriously, and when
the local procedure was exhausted, the shop stewards' committee
recommended strike action to a mass meeting of the workforce. The
vote was carried unanimously. The plant management – convinced
of their abilities to win the game of bluff and to use the vulnerability
of the Scotswood plant to their advantage – were surprised beyond
belief when the men walked out the gate: 'They never expected it.
They were convinced that we would never carry out the strike.
They got the shock of their lives when we actually walked out.'

As the strike began they made a crude attempt to reopen
negotiations:

One of their fellas came up to me and suggested we had a
meeting, you know. I had to point out to him that we had
followed the procedure right along the line and that we were
now on strike. If he wanted to call a meeting he would have
to do it in the correct manner and contact Georgie Arnold,
the Chairman of the Confed.

Scotswood was on strike! For the first time in living memory (with
the exception of nationally-called stoppages) the workers had
closed the plant through their collective action. The AUEW
District Committee officially supported the strike, but in the town
the informed opinion was that although the Scotswood lads had a
good case, they'd be lucky to win. And so it seemed. The company's
intransigence was one thing (as the strike broke Lord Robens
telegrammed Scotswood with the warning that the workers' action
was jeopardising the whole future of the plant); another was the
government's 10 per cent guidelines under phase three. In these
circumstances the company's offer of 9.3 per cent plus some

Shop Floor Voice

March/April. Price 5p   Newspaper of the Vickers National Shop Stewards Combine

SCOTSWOOD STRIKE IT RICH

IT WAS the 1977 Remembrance Day weekend and up and down Tyneside at the various ceremonies at Cenotaphs the buglers were sounding the traditional retreat. At Vickers Scotswood works that weekend had been chosen as start of their strike to advance their claim over improved wages and it was memorable because it was the first time in recent history that the Scotswood workers had commenced strike action over their domestic claim.

The negotiations on the claim had commenced several months rebefore as the anniversary date for claim was the 31st October. Feelings were running at at Scotswood because from a position of being of the leading factories the district for wages had slipped to being of the worst.

ombination of going a fixed wage system being caught up in the ment's pay policies cant that appren-served tradesmen king out a gross (£60.00) for forty with General on less than the claim had been through the re for the Industry with eration officials a failure to before the of the strike by the Shop Committee. had stood g the 10% in e claim for ed men pro bs.

On picket duty at Scotswood

set up to handle appeals, Social Security claims, premises and picketing. Teams of strikers in convoys of cars travelled the kngth and breadth of the Tyne to receive overwhelming support from shop stewards committees for their struggle. Heartening news came with the approval of the District Committee being given to the stoppage the official endorsement from the Executive Council arriving within a few days. The fastest approval that many members in the District can remember possibly the reason being that the EC member for the area had himself been a

Vickers Shop Steward many years ago.

The strike had been on for a fortnight and while morale was high, at the mass meetings there were unanimous votes for continuing the stoppage, progress in reaching a settlement was slow. Management had declined the strike committee's invitation to meet them in the working men's club but a compromise was reached when they agreed to meet in the foremen's club of the company premises. It was in this situation that a decision to call a meeting of all the Vickers stewards in the North East was taken. The move was

nothing new, for some time now the convenors of the local Vickers plants had been meeting montnly to swap notes and draw up claims and policies on what was going on in the works. This had been extended to a regular meeting of the shop stewards from the works at Elswick, Scotswood, Michell, Crabtrees Team Valley, Palmers Hebburn and the newly acquired Joyce Loebl. To a large extent the North East was the key part of the Vickers Shop Stewards' National Combine Committee and this was the time of show its strength. The meeting took place at the B Lg Hotel, Newcas-

and a packed meeting listened to the calls for immediate action to support Scotswood, debates on the best way of tackling the situation and eventually it was agreed that the various works committees approach their management and tell them that if a speedy settlement was not reached action would be taken by members of the rest of Vickers North East plants.

SYSTEM

The following Monday the strikers resumed work. From an average wage of £60.00 for forty hours for tradesmen they now had a guaranteed minimum of £72.75. Other grades pro data with the opportunity of making more on a bonus system and the wage in Februry has risen to £84.75 for the skilled 40 hours. In addition various improved conditions had been conceded, including free boots and overalls. With the solidarity expressed during the strike and with a victory under their belts organisation had strengthened in Scotswood. But the most important lesson of the strike has been that in the link up between the Vickers Shop Stewards and members in the various factories lies real trade union strenght.

LS

en made and once of the ut into isation nearby Club mittee mass week- were the and s of ere possible increase in bonus payment seemed near the limit. But informed opinion was turned on its head. The strike lasted through November to finish on the threshold of the Christmas holidays with a hurried negotiation and a settlement of around 22 per cent. As the *Shop Floor Voice* headlined: 'Scotswood Strike it Rich'. The earnings of the Scotswood workers had been restored to their earlier position in the league and they achieved one of the highest settlements made under phase three.

Many factors were involved in the success of the strike at Scotswood. Inside the factory the shop stewards committee (which covered most of the skilled workers as well as the unskilled and semi-skilled grades) had gained a great deal of experience in the previous four years. The discussions within the combine committee, and the success they had achieved in fighting off redundancy, all contributed to this. The committee was confident in its decision to take on Vickers management – a confidence which rested ultimately on the support they received from their members:

> From the beginning we had the members with us and we made a policy of keeping them informed on everything. And that continued during the strike. The one thing we were very emphatic about was that the members were kept well informed of what was going on and why they were on strike. That was the main success of the strike – communication. Before we went on strike we had mass meetings. We told every member that they were 'summons meetings', they'd get branched by their unions if they did not turn up.

No one was in any doubt about what was happening, or about what they were taking on. One man remembers how the chairman of the strike committee,

> really thrashed it into us. He said 'Let's be honest, when you're going out you're taking on the government, and you're not just taking on Scotswood, you're taking on Vickers House. Don't kid yourselves that it could be two or three weeks, it could be two or three months. We can't just go back for 50p after a week or so.' We knew what we were taking on alright. We were taking on the whole bloody lot of them.

In many respects the strike was a model of organisation. Mass meetings were held every week. At each, a register was taken of those in attendance. Each meeting contained detailed reports from shop stewards on every aspect of the strike's organisation (monies collected and spent, picket duties, support meetings etc.) and ended with a vote on the strike's continuance. Every steward had certain responsibilities on the various sub-committees that were set up. Throughout, the emphasis was upon 'involvement'. As the chairman of the strike committee put it: 'We said from the beginning that it was their strike; the members. We weren't going to tell them what to do and all that. That's why we had the vote every meeting. People had to be involved you see.'

A very well organised strike then: both efficient and democratic. Certainly one which took Vickers' management aback, and perhaps not what you'd expect from men taking strike action for the first time. However for the works committee, the strike was in many ways just an extension of their day to day struggles with management. As one of its members put it: 'We'd been involved in a lot of action supporting other people, taking action in our own sections, so it wasn't anything strange to go out of the door. The only thing that was new was getting in touch with outside bodies.'[2]

For all of its lack of strike experience, the shop steward organisation at Scotswood is well established; both in the plant and within Tyneside generally. Throughout 1977 in particular the committee had been involved in local campaigns to resist further redundancies in the area. And when they asked for support it was forthcoming:

> We've had support from every meeting we've been to. All the other stewards want to know is – 'have you kept procedure? Is the claim within the twelve months rule?' After that there were no problems. Financial collections and all the help they could give. It's been very good really.

Such local support is, of course, of great importance both financially (strikes cost quite a lot to run) and in terms of the morale of the people on strike. Strategically, however, the most important links were in the north-east Vickers plants, and these were organised in a sustained way.

Over the previous three years and within the context of establishing combine-level organisation, contact between the plants had been built up in a number of ways. The convenors and deputy convenors of each of the plants formed themselves into the North East Working Party, a committee which meets formally each month.[3] These meetings have agendas similar to those of the national combine meetings, and provide the opportunity for a detailed interchange of information on 'the state of the plants', as well as some kind of planning of future strategy. The shop stewards committees of all Vickers plants on Tyneside were well aware of the development of the Scotswood pay claim; they understood the claim and were able to anticipate the strike. As the strike broke, money was collected in every plant, sometimes through a compulsory fixed levy, sometimes through voluntary contributions:

> We had one or two people objecting to paying up but not many. Most of the people in our plant didn't need to have it explained to them. They knew the issue. All of us being employed by Vickers makes it easy to grasp, I think. It's pretty clear that we are in the same boat as the Scotswood lads and that we need to support them. As I said, most people paid without question.

But the support went beyond money. In 1977, in the wake of the Crabtree dispute, the North East Working Party broadened its base with the establishment of joint shop steward meetings. These meetings would be mass meetings of all shop stewards, they would meet twice yearly and could be called upon in the event of specific issues or a dispute. The Scotswood strike was just such a dispute, and in the second week of the strike a meeting was held in the Bridge Hotel in Newcastle. At this meeting the Scotswood convenor outlined the details of their claim and the strike; his account was then supported by the convenors of the other plants. A motion promising 'full moral and financial support' was passed after a discussion in which one-day strikes and an all-out stoppage were considered. The mood of the meeting was clear – moral support for the moment, but if that wasn't good enough there would be more militant action before the Scotswood lads were allowed to go to the wall.

The mood of the meeting at the Bridge Hotel was very clear to the people on the platform, and the Scotswood delegations were strengthened by it. It seems clear that something of it got through to

Vickers' management too. From a local incident the Scotswood strike had developed to the point where it could exert a major disruptive influence upon the company. As one convenor put it:

> They talk to each other, you know. In the gin-and-tonic half hours they talk about what's going on. And a manager in one division is not at all happy if something happening in another division is going to upset his production. I know that for a fact like. They don't like it. And that's a source of strength for us.

In November 1977 the men who worked at Scotswood were quite sure of this strength. As one of their shop stewards put it:

> The beauty of the strike for me was that the north east was solid; that was the beauty of it. At the meeting at the Bridge all the stewards made it known in no uncertain terms that if the strike was prolonged they would come out. Word of this would get back to Vickers House and they'd say 'God, this is going to spread, we'd better get this settled smart'.

And so it proved. The day after the meeting Scotswood management had its envoys driving around Tyneside in an attempt to contact and bring together the strike committee. After some delay (and a series of rather farcical incidents!) management and strikers arranged to meet on the neutral ground of the Vickers foremen's club, and after protracted negotiation management agreed to settle. The deal was taken back to the lads who – after a split vote – agreed to the terms and decided to return to work. Most people were pleased with the settlement and with the prospect of escaping a frugal Christmas.

> I voted against accepting the deal; the three of us did.
> Because I think if we'd held out we could have got *everything* we asked for. As it is we've got about £15. That's not bad. I accept the vote. The main people who voted to go back were blokes with families – kids to look after — and with Christmas coming up I can understand that. Personally I would have sooner carried on. I think you'll find that all the unmarried lads voted to carry on. But I've got no complaints. The strike was organised really well as far as I'm concerned.

The stewards made it clear that it was up to us; they weren't going to recommend one thing or another. That's good, I liked that. It was up to us and I accept the vote. £15 isn't bad.

In 1977 £15 was a good settlement. If they had stayed out longer they *may* have got a better deal, but one thing is clear – the combined support of all the north east plants was a vital factor in the settlement. Workers in a vulnerable plant like Scotswood, left isolated, could well have been on strike through Christmas and beyond, without any sort of settlement. In fact, such a strike could well have ended with the closure of the plant (this has been the all too common pattern in recent years). The success of the Scotswood strike therefore marks the success of co-ordinated, combine action. For the north east combine delegates it proved that combine action can work, that 'it can be done', and that the Scotswood strike has shown the way forward.

Within Scotswood itself the shop steward committee came out of the strike with a much stronger sense of purpose. They felt that at last they had turned the tables on the company; they felt, too, that the workers they represented appreciated the way they had organised the strike and now understood the significance of the Works Negotiating Committee, the North East Working Party, the combine committee, and all the other organisations that the shop stewards have set up and become involved in. As one of them put it:

It's difficult being a steward sometimes. There's so much that goes into it that the ordinary member doesn't realise. And you'll always have someone who thinks you're out for yourself. Getting money out of them can be difficult too 'What for? What do you do with it all?' . . . But after the strike their ideas were completely different, because they had seen at the mass meetings (with the reports and so on) the way things were organised, and the amount of work the committee does.

After the strike, contributions to the work funds doubled.

The failure of solidarity

Two successful strikes, then. But not all such attempts at co-ordinated action have such happy endings. The response to redundancy at Vickers Roneo in the spring of 1978 is a case in point.

At the beginning of May Vickers' management announced the closure of its toolroom at Romford and sent redundancy notices to the 61 toolroom workers. The reason for the closure was not shortage of work. The toolroom had a high level of overtime working and subcontracted some work. Neither was there a financial crisis. Vickers' intention was to sub-contract all its work. In the view of the toolroom workers, the plan was a rather sophisticated form of wage cutting – work being farmed out to small, low wage-paying factories. Even the local press agreed with this assessment of the situation, and urged Vickers to keep the toolroom open. Faced with this situation the shop stewards committee at Roneo, although at the time not affiliated to the combine committee, wrote a letter to the secretary of the combine which read:

> I am sorry for the inconvenience, but I feel that as you are an important member of Vickers Ltd., you should be aware of the situation at the Roneo Romford site.
>
> At this moment in time we are in the middle of a redundancy situation which would have been avoided if local management would have had prior consultation with the Shop Stewards' Committee. As it stands, through the bulldozing attitude of local management, we are now sitting on a time bomb which is not only damaging to the company but to the employees as well.
>
> I find the toolroom redundancies even harder to understand after the article in *Vickers Digest* in 1976 where Lord Robens states that our success nationally and internationally is vitally dependent upon skilled tradesmen.

The letter enclosed news cuttings and details of the redundancy situation. These details were communicated to all plants involved in the combine committee along with a request that 'every affiliated shop steward committee bring pressure to bear upon Vickers management in whatever way they see fit to stop the redundancies'. The letter gained a great deal of support. At South Marston, for example, workers were amazed at the situation:

> We've had a good few talks about it. It's incredible really, though, isn't it. Incredible. They're not closing it down

because there's not enough work, they're closing because
there's too much work! It's terrible really. You don't know
whether to laugh or cry.

The groundwork was being laid for a campaign of support. It was
not to be however. By the end of the month the redundancy was an
established fact.

The toolroom at Roneo was, after the closure of the steel factory,
the main basis of trade union organisation within the machine shop.
The toolroom workers were all skilled men a few of whom had
learned their trade unionism the hard way at Ford Dagenham. In
the toolroom they had organised tightly and effectively, controlling
the job and bargaining hard over their wage rates. In 1978 their rate
was one of the highest in the district. But this bargaining strength
was not established throughout the factory. In fact it contrasted
deeply with the kind of trade union organisation that existed in the
assembly areas. In this situation the exclusiveness of the toolroom
and the level of the wages paid there, bred suspicion and some
resentment – elements which were to contribute to a weakness as
the toolroom workers fought against the closure. In effect their own
past successes boomeranged against them. Management's propa-
ganda that the toolroom had priced itself out of existence was
listened to. Few of the production workers saw the fight against
closure to be *their* fight. Fewer than 200 of them (out of a work force
of over a thousand) attended a mass meeting called by the stewards.
Within the plant this first step toward mass support for the struggle
against the closure proved to be the last. Two days before the
second meeting of the combine committee's Southern Working
Party the toolroom workers met, reckoned to be on a looser and
voted to accept the closure and the redundancy money. Another
letter was written to the combine which informed the secretary
that:

Due to lack of support within Roneo we have made a
settlement with the management, this being one week's pay
for each year worked plus four weeks pay, also £500 if we
work normally up to the end of our notice . . . We would like
to thank you for your support. I only wish we had the same
support at Roneo. Please thank the brothers in the Combine
for their help.

This issue, taken alongside the disputes at Crabtree and Scotswood, illustrates the role that a combine committee can play within a company like Vickers. It also points to its weakness and makes clear the necessary inter-relationship between the organisation within the plants, the official union machinery (official union support was very important to the Scotswood workers) and the shop stewards committee structures established under the umbrella of the national combine committee.

Chapter 11

The Problem of Unity

The shop stewards' combine committee is an established part of the shop stewards' organisation within Vickers. What is not yet clear is how this committee will develop in the years ahead. In this, active combine committee members (as well as members of some of the non-affiliated shop stewards committees) are aware of a number of problems and dilemmas; issues which are not peculiar to Vickers but relate generally to the problem of building rank-and-file organisations within the corporate sector. To many people it appears as 'the problem of unity'.

In July 1977, with the experience of the Vickers Crabtree dispute behind them, the convenors of the four Vickers plants on Tyneside called the first of a series of twice yearly shop stewards' meetings. The first was held at the County Hotel in Newcastle and was attended by some eighty shop stewards from the Elswick, Scotswood, Michell Bearing and Crabtree works. The platform speakers included the plant convenors, white collar representatives from the 'staff unions', TASS and APEX, and the convenor from the local Parsons factory. The meeting focused on the run-down of Tyneside and of Vickers in particular. Throughout the evening 'unity' was a central theme – unity 'to combat what Vickers is doing in the north east'. The spokesman from the Michell Bearings plant put it like this:

> Unity is strength. If we stick together we might get
> somewhere. Vickers split you up in order to divide you. I
> know it's a hard job but as long as we remain split up into
> little fragments we're allowing them to do it to us.

A point that was echoed by the white collar representative from TASS:

In the past manual workers wouldn't co-operate with the staff, and the staff didn't like manual unions. But people are now realising the importance of individual unions within the plants working together. We can all see that local management can't make decisions; that all the top decisions are made by London people. We should demand to know what are the policies of Vickers toward the North East. It's about time these people (the Weinstock's of the world) were told that we're not going to tolerate their wealth and power saying where people will work or won't work. The more the staff and the shops get together the better the chance of getting some answers from London.

So 'unity' is the key – unity between plants and unity within the plants. The two strikes on Tyneside achieved some sort of unity. But at Scotswood the boilermakers worked through the strike, as did the members of the staff unions. At Romford the support of the combine was not matched within the plant. So it's worth asking just how big a problem is this search for 'unity', especially in the national (and multi-national) context?

The size of the problem

The short answer, of course, is that it is an extremely difficult problem. The existence of companies like Vickers means that workers require a form of rank-and-file unity very different from those upon which the trade union movement has been built in the past. In the past unity has depended upon the existence of certain things in common: a locality or a trade; producing the same product or being up against the same management in negotiations. Today none of these are sufficient. In the context of a company which straddles the length of the country – from Clydeside to Brighton and across from Thetford in Norfolk to Swindon in Wiltshire and the rest of the world besides – a trade-, plant- or region-based unity is insufficient in itself. The question of unity within Vickers raises the issue of working class unity itself, and in answering it we, of necessity, touch upon some of the major issues that face working class organisation in the 1980s.

The distribution of Vickers' plants in Britain

The move toward combine committee organisation within Vickers was associated with the company's change-over from an armaments producer to a multi-national conglomerate producing a wide range of products from a number of divisions, selling in a variety of different markets. Vickers' fastest growing markets are in office equipment, which involves mainly assembly and light pressing work in the London area, in Liverpool and in France. Another new growth area is in lithographic plates which again involves semi-skilled labour operating continuous (24 hour) automated chemical processes. In addition the Offshore Developments Group employs glass-fibre construction workers and advanced design staff. These diverse activities have little in common with each other or with the mechanical engineering group which forms the core of the 'old Vickers'. The plants in this latter group however do have a little more in common: there is considerable movement of work between them, earnings are more immediately comparable, shifts in world trade have a broadly similar effect. Within this group only machine tool production at Kearney and Trecker Marwin and, for different reasons, the heavy engineering plant at Scotswood, are significantly different. Not surprisingly it is in this group that combine organisation is most advanced.

The composition of the labour force

There is more to this diversity than products, divisions and markets. The changes which Vickers has gone through over the past ten years or so has also affected the *composition* of its labour force. Traditionally (that is pre-Suez) Vickers has been the employer of male, skilled, well organised, trade union labour – the so-called 'labour aristocrats'. Tyneside – where the boilermakers still have their national head office – is one of the homes of skilled trade unionism in Britain. And Vickers was a basis for this. The modern Vickers is very different. While the company still prides itself on being a leading engineering concern, its labour force is now preponderantly (and increasingly) involved in routine production work – the arena of the 'semi-skilled' worker. For the Vickers' work force as a whole it has been a case of 'dilution through take-over'. The take-over of Roneo Vickers added over a thousand semi-skilled workers to the pay roll, Howson Algraphy a further 1,500 and more were brought in by takeovers of Fanfold, Middows, Four Plus and Hirst Buckley. KTM and Hasties are examples of take-overs that have brought in skilled workers but they do not alter the general picture of the 'old' and 'new' Vickers; a picture which can be understood by contrasting Scotswood with Romford. The Newcastle plant has a manual labour force of 550. Every one of these production workers are men and 63 per cent of them are skilled. At Romford in contrast, even *before* the closure of the toolroom, just 18 per cent of the manual labour force was skilled – the rest being predominantly semi-skilled, women workers.

But skill, and the kind of jobs that people do, is just one aspect of the changing composition of the labour force at Vickers. Another (and closely related) aspect has to do with the kind of traditions and organisations which workers have built up over the years. This is another dimension within which the change of the Old to the New Vickers can be appreciated. At the time of the first world war, in the days when over 57,000 people worked at Elswick and Scotswood on the Tyne, the workers in these factories established one of the first workshop organisations in England with a formal agreement, full negotiating rights and a full-time convenor. This was all established by skilled men in a time of good trade. In Barrow and on Tyneside the stability of Vickers' position made it 'a good employer', offering both managers and workers a lifetime's employment. Numerous articles in *Vickers News* report on the retirement dinners that have taken place in these towns. In May 1966, for example, an account is given of five managers at Barrow who retired with a total of 224 years service to the company; also present at the dinner was Alderman G. E. Connell, MBE, Chairman of the Barrow Watch Committee, who had retired in 1962 after 44 years as a machinist in the boiler shop. By all accounts this experience of security fostered amongst the workforce of the 'old Vickers' a sense of identity with the firm. So much was this the case that, to quote one steward: 'When we first started having redundancies here a lot of the workers wouldn't blame Vickers – they thought it was the government's fault. They should be fighting more wars!'

The close connection between Vickers and national war mobilisations also helped produce amongst many of the workers a strong patriotism. The Elswick works was not only the home of one of the

June 7th, 1920.

Sir W. G. Armstrong, Whitworth & Co., Ltd.,
Elswick Works, Newcastle-on-Tyne.

Provisions for Dealing with Shop Questions.

1. Workpeople employed in the Establishment shall have Representatives selected from the Members of their Trade Unions employed in the Establishment, to act on their behalf, in accordance with the terms of this Agreement.

2. The Representatives shall be known as Shop Stewards.

3. The appointment of such Shop Stewards shall be determined by the Trade Unions concerned and each Trade Union may have such Shop Stewards.

4. The names of the Shop Stewards, their Trade Union and the shop or portion of a shop in which they are employed, shall be intimated officially on election to the Firm by the Trade Union concerned.

S.S. 10,833

first shop stewards committees, but also of a complete battery of volunteer officers and men of the 1st Northumberland Volunteer Artillery Brigade, who fought in the South African War as 'The Elswick Battery'. And it was not so long ago that the shop stewards at Elswick invited management to their annual dinner and united with them in a toast to the monarch.

Many things have changed since the war. What now remains on Tyneside is a deep rooted trade unionism held together by a pride in the idea that Tyneside workers set the pace within the engineering industry. All this perhaps dates back to the 1898 strike for the eight hour day. The presence of this tradition was certainly felt at Scotswood in 1977 when the workers there (for all their vulnerability) refused to work for a cut rate.

But there is more to all this than pride. The tradition of craft trade unionism on Tyneside has handed down shop floor organisations of considerable power. In Scotswood and Elswick the workers take for granted an organisational foundation which, in most other Vickers plants, has either been lost, or is still being struggled for. While the convenor at Thetford keeps his papers in the locker by his machine and while workers at Kearney and Trecker Marwin have to deal with a situation where management allowed full-time convenor facilities only to withdraw them a few months later, stewards at Elswick and Scotswood have never known a time when there was no full-time convenor or works committee office. Shop floor organisation in these plants is also strengthened by a very high ratio of stewards to members: at Scotswood, in the engineering section there are 26 shop stewards for about 300 members, a ratio of one to twelve. At the Roneo Vickers factory in Romford, a thousand workers are represented by just six shop stewards – one steward for every 166 members.

These 'facilities' are not managerial favours but rather the legacy of past struggles. A legacy which is further represented in the controls which the shop steward organisation is able to exercise over the day-to-day decisions within the plant. At Scotswood management's attempt to introduce a new system of job timings met with the men's refusal to work with the time study experts. The scheme was eventually abandoned. At Elswick and Scotswood the works committee controls both the extent and the allocation of all overtime working in the factory. This strength – the degree of autonomous control which the committees are able to exercise over the day-to-day life of the factory – is bolstered by their ability to build up a source of independent financing. At both these plants the practice of imposing a financial levy upon every member dates back to before the First World War, and forms a basis for the shop stewards' committee fund. And there are additional sources of finance. The men who work in the plants are able to purchase boots and shoes at a discounted price: these are sold through the shop stewards committee, not through one of the management's departments. One consequence of this is that the convenors' offices bear a close resemblance to an emporium: discussions of combine committee policy are interspersed not only with phone calls from the press, management, and other shop stewards, but also by members trying on this and that shoe and discussing the likelihood of other, preferred styles being available. This development into retailing was carried a step further when the Elswick shop stewards organised the sale of pots and pans to provide the initial float for the combine committee newspaper.

The strength of this organisational structure, taken together with the locality of Tyneside and the ever-present memories of the past, has succeeded in building up a strong sense of local class solidarity within the factories. As one steward put it:

> I've been offered promotion a few times. I'm not interested in it you understand, politically I'm not interested in joining sides with them buggers. But I've told them 'If I take promotion off you it would ruin my social life.' They don't understand, but it would. I'd lose all my friends if I took one of those jobs. I wouldn't be able to go into the club.

This sense of solidarity is reinforced in the plants by a very low turnover of labour. The north east generally has a low level of immigration into the area, and in the Vickers plants the labour force is largely composed of men who were born in the area and have worked for the company for many years. In this context the shop stewards' expectation that their members behave 'like trade unionists' is reinforced by the committee's power, and accepted right, to discipline erring members. During the Scotswood strike, remember, a register was kept of all those in attendance. Absence left the member open to disciplinary measures at the branch meeting. During those strike meetings, the speakers from the platform answered all questions, knowing the name of the questioner, the shop in which he worked, his trade, and his background.

The contrast between this and the situation in some of the other Vickers plants is quite marked. As one southern TGWU shop steward observed:

> It's different with the craft unions. I've had a few discussions
> with a bloke who's a shop steward in SOGAT. Well they
> have the powers to *fine* people who don't attend branch
> meetings. Well we don't have powers like that. I'm not
> sure if I agree with it either, but it does make for a totally
> different situation.

The measure of this difference became clear during a discussion at one of the National Combine Committee meetings. The shop stewards committee at Romford had decided to affiliate to the national combine. Such affiliation requires an annual fee of £5 and some kind of funding to support the expenses of delegates who attend the meetings. The Romford shop stewards committee had no funds of its own. As a result the shop stewards decided to take a collection on the shop floor specifically aimed at the need to affiliate to the combine committee. The collection produced £10 and, disheartened, the shop stewards sent the money as a donation to the combine, with a letter recording their regret at being unable to play an active part in the affairs of the national committee. In the discussion of this letter a delegate from the north east argued:

> I think they're taken a wrong decision there, like. I think
> they've got very disheartened by the response of the
> membership. But you've got to be hard with the workers on
> some occasions. In our plant we'll threaten to stop the
> overtime if we don't get their support on an issue like this.

Probably the shop stewards at Romford were wrong to become so disheartened, but the situation there is different in so many ways from that of the north east: a large mass-production plant with a high rate of labour turnover, and a female labour force which has not been steeped in the traditions of the trade union movement. These workers have their ways of resisting the boss in the factory but it is not a way which has led them to build a durable organisation.

Where such an organisation has developed it has either, as in the case of the print workers, isolated itself, or, as in the case of the steel factory, been destroyed by Vickers.

This variation between *plants* is compounded by stark variations between *grades* of workers employed by the company. In the old Vickers plants the manual/staff divide has always been an important one. The distinction was established through the power of the foreman to hire and fire labour and through the financial rewards and status which accompanied promotion. In the north eastern plants the foremen were always company men, organised away from unions in the company's Foreman's Association. But in these plants things have changed in this respect too. Run-down and closure has not only threatened manual workers. Office and supervisory staff have also begun to join trade unions. An APEX representative notes that:

> The old idea that management would look after the staff who they worked with is a dead duck. Most of us have realised that we must have some organised trade union to look after our interest. This really came to us around 1970 by which time our wages were falling well behind. The next break through came with the Equal Pay Act; the women's hopes were raised by that, and joining the union seemed the only way of getting anything done about it.

Unionised white collar workers in the north eastern plants have attempted to build links with those on the factory floor. The experience at Scotswood with the corporate committee (see chapter 6) was important here. There is now talk of a similar committee at Elswick.

> We were prompted by the success of the corporate committee at Scotswood. This was brought together at a time of crisis but wise men ought to foresee what might happen – God forbid that it should happen at Elswick, but why wait for a crisis, only to be disorganised when it first hits you?

These developments, while important, do not evaporate the differences which people have 'traditionally' felt divide the office from the factory floor. Some shop stewards still complain that they never know what an office worker earns: 'It's all done individually with them fellas. They're not prepared to come in with us and bargain over wages.' The office representatives are aware of 'suspicion'; aware too of the fact that 'Shop floor workers have had to fight for their rights over the years, whereas office workers haven't had to put so much effort into being trade unionists.' In spite of all this, though, things are changing. They are changing in other parts of the company, too – but in a rather different way.

Vickers, remember, ran down its design teams in the engineering division during the 1950s. As a consequence Elswick and Scotswood employ comparatively few technical staff. Within the new Vickers these highly trained technical workers have tended to become 'divisionalised' apart from the manual workers. This happened, to some extent, with the Oceanics group; the tendency is seen most clearly in the formation of a Design and Procurement Division (D and P). This division employs almost no manual workers. It was based on the South Marston site in Swindon for some years (it has since been moved – with personnel – to Eastleigh) but during that time the workers in the Hydraulics Division had almost no contact with D and P staff:

> We could never find out anything about that place. We could
> never find out whether there was subcontracting going on
> that we could be doing. We didn't have any contact with the
> staff there. The way we were separated, it was like being in a
> different country!

This last point raises, yet again, the important role played by the company in this question of unity. In contrasting the north east with the south, as we have done, there is a danger that we never get past the appearance of things. Elswick is certainly different from Romford today, but in 1965 a strong shop stewards' organisation existed at the steel factory in Romford. Vickers closed it down. At Swindon one of the older stewards often laments on the changes in trade union organisation he has observed in his life time:

> I had worked in the railway workshops in Swindon and there
> were some real unionists there, I can tell you: coppersmiths,
> sheetmetal workers. The AUEW, and in fact all unions, had
> first-class stewards and convenors and this in turn produced
> good union officials. Dick Pearce, the old AUEW district

secretary, was without a doubt, in my opinion, the best union official Swindon has ever had. My old man was an active trade unionist. He had a fantastic library. He knew all about the union and all about socialism. He read and he educated himself for the union, to fight the employer. But the sort of shop steward we're getting today, most of them won't put in any time at all – unless it's paid for.

In Swindon the closure of the railway shops and the re-organisation of Vickers put an end to many of these traditions. The Hydraulics Division at South Marston was built in large part upon agricultural and general workers who were trained, not by way of an apprenticeship, but 'on the machine'. Unlike 'time-served' men their status as skilled workers is specific to Vickers, and this dependance has been at the root of much of their reluctance to 'push the company too far'.

The fabric of the company and the strategy of its management has an important effect upon the composition of the labour force and the problems faced in building unity within it. This is made no clearer – and with no greater irony – than in the case of the north east itself. For if these plants mark the strongest centre of shop floor trade unionism within the Vickers' empire, they are also the plants which have been subjected to the most severe and consistent job loss. The extent of this irony has not been lost on the workers who work in these plants: they are aware of the threat, a threat which is posed to (and to an extent provoked by) their way of life. It is for this reason that the shop stewards in the north eastern plants have been most consistent in their search for a united front through the combine. They have learned to be patient (and occasionally generous) with shop stewards' organisations that differ so markedly from their own. They have also been forced to shift out of their localism, to see themselves in a national (and international) context; and in this – as we shall see in part four – they have tentatively questioned the established limits of the old trade unionism that has been handed down to them. Before turning to those broader matters it is important that we consider a further aspect of the problems which face the people who are attempting to build unity around a combine committee organisation at Vickers: the problem of their relationship with the official trade union organisations of which they are members.

Unity and 'the unions'

As an engineering company Vickers has always been a member of the Engineering Employers' Federation. As a member of the Federation it negotiates a nationally agreed basic wage and adheres to the disputes procedure agreed with the Confederation of Shipbuilding and Engineering Unions (the 'Confed'). Local plant bargaining takes place within this framework. But this only applies to the *engineering* plants. While the Old Vickers was covered by this one national agreement the new Vickers embraces four different industries, and has joined the relevant employers federation in each of them. As a consequence the national agreements of the furniture industry, the printing industry and the building industry apply to particular parts of the company – different national agreements and also different trade unions. Within the Engineering Group bargaining is conducted through the unions of the Confed. At Slingsby the workers are members of the construction workers union, UCATT; at Howson Algraphy the National Graphical Association (NGA) has a closed shop; at the Dartford and Romford assembly plant most of the labour force are in the TGWU. The complicated nature of these arrangements can be seen as a further source of fragmentation within the Vickers labour force. It is also one of the strongest arguments for a different form of trade union organisation within the company – one which unites the whole workforce. This has been the claim of the Vickers combine committee, and the response it has received from the official union structures has been – at best – ambiguous.

This ambiguity finds its clearest expression in the AUEW's policy on combine committees. This raises,

> No objections to regular meetings of combine committees or to the adoption of constitutions by committees, [but] there must be no attempt to charge expenses against the union. There must also be no attempt to take over the functions of any of the properly constituted bodies in the union, with respect to policy-making, national negotiations or the powers of the District Committees on the regulation of wages or conditions, or for example, the control of overtime.

Combine committees can meet but they cannot call upon the

support of the union; they can expect no financial assistance; nor can they involve themselves in negotiations. While, on the one hand, the union recognises the real need for shop stewards to be in detailed contact with their opposite numbers in the other plants, they are, on the other, unsure about the consequences of such organisation for their own positions and for the balance of power within the District. It was this same logic which in 1969, in the face of a total stoppage at Ford, led Jim Conway (then General Secretary of the AUEW) to comment: 'These men are just convenors, and they have no negotiating rights whatsoever. My own view is that the officials of the unions involved have accepted the agreement and that's that.'[1]

The strength of the case for the combine committee is that it provides a more effective means of dealing with the giant corporations. This is a logic which, if carried through, could involve a radical change in the structure of British trade unionism. The official union structures are concerned in the support they presently give to the combine principle, that these changes be kept under control. Management (for somewhat different reasons) share this concern. In the context of Vickers the emergence of company-wide negotiations involving a combine-wide shop stewards committee would mark a radical – and threatening – departure. This threat finds expression in the behaviour of the union officials. To quote a combine committee delegate:

It seems clear to me that the combines are the way forward. It's difficult for trade unionists to oppose the principle of combine committees. You cannot oppose the principle. What happens in practice is different, though. In its practical application the officials aren't interested. They know what's best for us.

All these problems became clear when Vickers decided to introduce a new pension scheme for its employees. At Vickers (as in other companies) the kind of fringe benefits which the company makes available to its employees has been a perennial source of distinction between manual workers and those 'on the staff'. One of the conditions of service for white collar workers within the company is that they contribute to the company's pension scheme, the combination of their payments and the company's being the basis for a Vickers pension. Traditionally, the manual workers have not been offered such a scheme – on retirement they have always been entirely dependent upon state pensions. Recent revision of the state pension scheme has, paradoxically, made the provision of an occupational pension scheme much more attractive to the employers. As a result the last four years have witnessed the widespread introduction of such schemes.

From the point of view of a large company the efficiency of a pension scheme (apart from the tax advantages) is linked to the size of the pension fund. Equally the establishment and management of such a fund necessitates a certain degree of co-operation from the workforce and, as consequence, some kind of discussion and negotiation with the trade unions *at a company level*. At Vickers this involved discussions with certain national officials of the unions, the setting up of the pension scheme (with agreed contributions and benefits) and the selection of trade union trustees for the pension fund. All this was carried out in London. There was no discussion with the workers in the plants and no member of the AUEW (the majority union representing manual workers in the company) was selected as a trustee. The matter was signed and sealed as a *fait accompli*.

This situation revealed the vulnerability of the combine committee. Without total coverage of the plants, and with some plants represented at the combine meetings by delegates other than the plant convenor, they were wide open to a flanking movement. The committee met in mid-1974, however, and decided, that the situation had to be corrected: 'It's our money, our members contributions, our bloody pensions and we don't have a say in it. Who the hell are they to sign up for us anyway?'

Some plant delegates argued that the combine committee should call a national strike against the pension agreement. Others – more realistic – argued that the committee should recommend that all plant shop steward committees advise their members against joining the pension scheme until satisfactory negotiations and representation had been established. The officers of the combine committee were instructed to meet the relevant national officials and argue for a full and proper discussion of the scheme with representatives of shop floor workers: 'We went down there to Transport House, and they wouldn't see us. They refused to see us.

Vickers New Pension Scheme
is it a good one ?

Yes·If ! ! ! you are a 64 years old widower
with four kids under ten ! ! !

We had to force our way in to a meeting. Force our way in and shout at them.'

This intervention wasn't too successful but at least it had the effect of producing a National Delegate Conference to be held in the Great Western Hotel in London. The conference and its organisation is remembered with real bitterness by those combine committee delegates who attended:

> Right up to the last minute nobody knew who was paying for the rail tickets. As an official conference the union or the company should be paying the fares. But we couldn't find out right up to the last minute. I spent days ringing around all the different unions, one thing from this one, a different thing from another one.

The combine committee delegates arrived early for the meeting and distributed leaflets on every seat explaining the nature of the committee, the stand they had taken on the pension scheme and their role in the setting up of the Delegate Conference. These were all removed before the Conference began!

> There were all union officials on the platform. The APEX bloke was in the chair and he just ran the meeting his way. He wouldn't call us to speak. There was no real discussion at all; some of the officials fell asleep!

The conference carried the official line. As an organised force the combine committee had been out-manoeuvred. On the first issue involving company-wide bargaining the full time officials held on to the reigns tightly indeed. For many it left a bitter taste. It also served to pose clearly the nature and the extent of the problem they faced in Vickers.

Chapter 12

The Organisation of a Combine Committee

The people who are active in the formation and development of the combine committee within Vickers know that they face a lot of problems. The last chapter was based upon their direct experiences and discussions. For the most part these people are shop stewards with a considerable amount of experience as union activists within their factories and unions: as a group they tend to be people who have been involved in a variety of other issues (through the trades councils, district committees, and local campaigns) which have taken them outside the confines of plant level negotiations. If one thing binds them together it is the belief – often stated at the Leeds meetings – that working men and women face similar problems which benefit from being discussed and acted on together. They feel, too, that the combine committee structure offers an important vehicle for such communication and also has the possibility of becoming an effective weapon for achieving some successes. Often they express doubts; sometimes the problems seem insuperable. In such moments they rely upon a basic belief that:

> The important thing is to keep the combine in existence. As long as we can keep it moving along, keeping the plants informed; as long as we are here, meeting regularly we are the basis for something. That's what I feel we must do – to keep the combine.

Most often they feel that they are making progress, and that there are ways of building a rank-and-file committee which brings together workers throughout the new Vickers. In this they see the combine committee to be but one part of a more general struggle; an important part, nevertheless, and one that can be strengthened in a number of ways.

The problem of structure

The ambiguity which many union officials feel toward combine committees is often shared by shop stewards and their members. Delegates to the combine committee talk of the problem of getting people to 'think beyond the plant'.

> We used to run collections, you know – for the firemen and so on, when they were on strike. People would give, like, but there was always a little bit of 'what's this to do with us', sort of thing. When we started talking about the combine we met the same reaction – 'What are they up to now? We've hardly got an organisation here and they're talking about combines.' They knocked us back on the first vote but we argued, like – the advantages of being in touch with the other plants – and we won the day.

The combine committee has recognised that the question of 'interference' in the affairs of affiliated plant committees is a delicate problem. So the combine grouping is a loose one, based upon the autonomy of the individual plant committees; it has accepted that the national combine cannot *instruct* the workers or shop stewards of any plant to follow a particular line of action. It can offer information, support and, on specific policy issues, recommendations that particular lines of action be taken.[1]

While this approach has worked tolerably well at Vickers, real problems have been created by the unevenness of the development of the committee throughout the company. Its main strength is still within the Engineering Group, particularly in the plants along the Tyne, and there are voices which argue that the combine should settle with what its got and build on that:

> It seems obvious to me we have to stick together – but in the north east we can do something. It's a waste of time trying to involve some of these other plants. Half of them are not trade unionists. If we stick with our strengths up here we may get somewhere.

The majority view however, is in disagreement. For one thing most of the stewards take a less critical view of the workers in the other plants. Their most telling argument, however, rests on the nature of the company:

> It's all very well saying we should go on our own, on a group
> basis if you like, or on the basis of the north east. But all the
> plants are in the same company. They all come under Vickers
> House. That's where the decisions about the money are taken.
> And if we're not all in the combine they will always be able
> to play one plant off against the other. We have to go forward
> together. We need a *national* combine.

The committee has, pragmatically, developed a structure which
bridges these views. Increasingly *regional* groupings are being seen
as the first points where shop floor action can be coordinated. The
North East Working Party and its attendant joint shop stewards
meetings is the best example of the potential for such sub-
groupings. This Northern Group (which aims to expand to include
the two Scottish plants) has encouraged the formation of other
groupings based upon 'the south' and Yorkshire. These regional
committees offer the possibility of bridging the three months
between national combine meetings in Leeds. They have the
practical advantage of minimising transport costs for delegates, and
– for the southern plants – they combat any idea that the combine is
simply 'a northern outfit'. More generally they can be seen as
groupings which allow people to make adjustments between the
increasingly multi-national nature of capital and the (as always)
local nature of their own experiences. People (unlike capital)
live in places; and places develop different traditions, different ways
of doing things – they have a different 'feel' about them. The
dominance of capital means that shop stewards' organisations need
to have links with all other plants in the company; workers need
some kind of national organisation of their own to develop any
semblance of a strategy. But equally the consequences of the
company's policy are felt in particular localities. And local unity (of
workers in, and beyond, the company) is an important basis for
action. Combine committees are an important part of a working class strategy for this new phase of capitalist development;
but they are only a part of it. The regional committees within the
Vickers combine committee, linking the workforce with other
workers in the company and the area, are an early attempt to
reconcile these aspects of the present situation.[2]

Spreading the combine

The regional committees are important, but they do not offer any complete solution to the 'problem of unity' and the uneven development of trade union organisation within the company. The committee's aim is still to spread the combine's organisation throughout the company – to involve all the plants and all grades of workers. At each meeting at Leeds delegates discuss the number of plants represented at the meeting, the reason for certain delegates not arriving, the possibility of others coming to the next meeting. As a practical means of encouraging attendance, a pooled fare system (whereby the under-financed committees and those who have to travel long distances to Leeds are subsidised by the others) was introduced. And the national committee meetings have been made attractive in other ways. In 1977 a delegate from Thetford put forward the argument for expanding the meetings into occasional weekend schools:

> I look at it like this. We spend most of Friday travelling. We drink on Friday night, have the meeting on Saturday morning and off again – another five hour journey. It's a bit mad really. If we arranged a proper weekend we could discuss things more at our leisure without rushing off with a hangover. And, let's face it, the weekend is the only time a bloke gets with his family. His wife might like to come along if we organised something in a residential centre.

The principle was accepted. At six monthly intervals the combine meets for the weekend at a hall of residence in the University of Leeds. The meetings include the normal business of the combine together with open discussion sessions. In December 1977 shop stewards from Ford and Lucas Electrical led a discussion on the question of combine committee organisation. After the session a young delegate from the Crabtree plant in Gateshead spoke for a lot of people when he said:

> It's been really great this weekend. I'm learning something new all the time. You know it's good to be away from the plant and meeting and listening to people who've had a lot more experience than you've had. I've learned a lot here already.

The food was good too!

These developments are important, but clearly the central concern of the national committee is that it establish its relevance to the workers on the shop floors of the various Vickers plants. This necessity has been argued clearly by Henry Friedman (an ex-convenor of the River plant at Dagenham) in an issue of the WEA's *Studies of Trade Unionists*.[3]

> One can note from experience that workers in a factory
> making car components do not feel that they have anything in
> common with a factory making aircraft components just
> because the two factories are owned by the same combine.
> Yet clearly they do have a common interest and it is up to the
> combine committee to prove this to the workforce. In this
> respect the keyword is 'relevance' and the combine committee
> must be made to be relevant to the workers on the shop floor.
> A vital element in this is building up rank-and-file
> involvement in the decision-making process. This means a
> constant flow of information both ways between the
> committee and the membership. But not only information,
> which after all means power, but also the extensive use of mass
> meetings of all trade union members in the plant, and regular
> report-back sessions from combine committee meetings. In
> this way the combine organisation is able to take workers
> beyond the narrow, sectional outlook of the plant and show
> the relevance of a national and overall perspective for the
> combine in which they work.

Such a comprehensive pattern of report-back meetings, infor-mation and discussion has not been established consistently within the Vickers combine, and one of the early delegates (the ex-convenor of Water Lane) sees this to be a major problem in the present stage of the committee's growth:

> It's no good shop stewards attending combine committee
> meetings if the decisions are not communicated. That's the
> stage I was at, at first, before the closure of Water Lane, trying
> to make sure the decisions percolate down to the shop floor.
> You can't expect if a problem arises at Swindon or Elswick to
> be able to go to the shop floor and say 'Look there's a problem

at Swindon and we've decided on the combine committee to
support them' and get any response just like that. You've first
got to show the lads over a period of time that the combine
plays a leading role in day-to-day business. At Water Lane
we got support for a one day strike over the pensions issue.
But that was only possible because leading up to it we'd built
up a dialogue between the membership and the combine
committee.

The combine committees represent a new (and untested) form of
organisation. Unlike the plant-based committee, there is no overlap
between the combine committee and the branch and local committees of the union. For this reason there needs to be new ways of
doing things. At the very least, old ways need to be re-examined.

For the Vickers' shop stewards, the publication of a regular
quarterly combine committee newspaper – *Shop Floor Voice* – was
seen as an important step in this direction. The paper's first issues
appeared in the spring of 1978. Financed by the sale of pots and
pans, and sometimes delivered by lorry drivers from plant to plant,
it made an impact. A delegate from a southern plant put it like this:

Management didn't like it. You could tell that. Personally I
hope the newspaper will improve, and I honestly think it will.
But irrespective of what was in it management didn't like it.
They didn't like the idea of the combine committee being
able to produce a newspaper. You know what I mean?
They've liked to treat us as a bit of a joke, I think. After that
they got quite nasty about it. Which is good. It shows they're
worried when they get nasty.

It was helpful on the shop floor, too, as a shop steward from
Tyneside notes:

I took copies of the newspaper and I took them and sold one
to every one of my members. I told them 'read that'. It was
useful you know to have something from the combine,
something to give people that they could look at and talk
about.

The newspaper was not read with universal agreement. Many
people had criticisms to make of it; but it has already generated

more discussion (and 'letters to the editor') than its competitor – *Vickers News*.

The newspaper is an important arm of the combine committee in its attempt to establish itself as a negotiating force within the company. To do this however the official union – company contact has to be broken; the combine committee has to initiate issues; it has to prove itself capable of winning something. A steward from Crabtree's in Gateshead stated this forcefully:

> It must achieve something for everyone in Vickers. They've got to set an objective and win it. I think sick leave is the most important thing now. Through the combine at the moment we just pick each others' brains, and gain each others' advantages, we don't achieve any advance together. We've failed on the pensions scheme but we could get somewhere on the sick pay scheme. If the combine did that it would be made.

The combine committees that have extended beyond the stage of exchanging information have done so via an organised campaign around specific targets. This is the case today at Lucas where the Alternative Plan has taken on central importance; at Ford the parity campaign galvanised the plants together; and so too at Leyland where the demand to 'open the books' was combined with other clearly set objectives. In this context Henry Friedman has noted that while the Leyland committee was set up with the limited objective of exchanging information in the 1960s it,

> Began to set itself long term goals in terms of the 40 hour week, £1 an hour, and higher pensions, all of which were achieved by the combined strength of the whole Leyland committee. The long-term aims such as the 40-hour week were vigorously pursued with marches through London and other big cities and mass lobbies of Parliament and the Employers' Federation. The demands and decisions of the combine committee were also advanced in union branches, trades councils, etc. as a way of adding more pressure and receiving more support throughout the trade union movement.[4]

The Vickers combine committee has begun a low key campaign on the issue of sickness pay and some shop stewards now feel that this should be extended to the question of a minimum wage within the company. But if one thing has become clear to the people active in the combine committee it is that workers have no control over – or even access to – the centre of the company. And it is at the centre (the banker) where the key life and death decisions are made. As things stand at the moment any information the people who work in the plants receive on their future livelihood comes bit by bit through 'the grapevine'. 'Secret rooms' keep people's futures locked away. The plans for a particular plant are unknown to the people who will be affected most by them. The closure of plants; redundancies and automation; nationalisation and compensation – all are elements in a situation which raise *investment* to the centre of the stage. The 'hidden costs' discussed in chapter three and the 'problem of unity' examined in this chapter all relate to a company which is organised and controlled by people other than those who work in its factories. It is this fact which has led the combine committee to examine and support policies which fall beyond the traditional realm of trade union activity, to consider the kind of *long-term strategies* that need to be followed by working class organisations in the age of the giant corporations.

Part 4

STRATEGIES AND COUNTER-STRATEGIES

At Vickers Ltd., the workers and their shop stewards committees have, in spite of all the difficulties, established contact with each other; information is exchanged between plant committees and a framework has been established for the development of a company-wide rank-and-file committee. But what of the future? This last part of the *Workers' Report* examines the prospects which face the committee, and it begins by shifting our attention, once again, to the company.

In part one we saw how the giant corporations have developed quite detailed accounting techniques with which to plan and chart their global developments; we saw how Vickers, under the direction of Matthews, has developed similar business techniques. It is important now to remember that the corporations also have plans for the people who work for them – their 'labour'. These plans are equally sophisticated, detailed and thought-out. Certainly the corporate bosses think about trade unionism a great deal. They meet and discuss the problems of combine committees and the advantages involved in the various industrial relations policies. Chapter 13 examines the kinds of strategies which are being developed within the corporate sector to deal with labour problems. It is against this background that the final chapter of the *Report* examines the policies which could be developed to counter corporate power and the role that combine committees might play in this process.

Chapter 13

Regulating Labour

Since the war the giant corporations have been increasingly concerned with 'the problem of labour', a problem which is rooted in the indispensibility of the men and women who tend the machines on the factory floor. The plants will not run without workers (as the *Sunday Times* noted 'the bionic worker' has yet to be produced) and while they can be fitted in to the corporate accounting scheme – as 'labour costs', 'natural wastage' and so on – 'labour' is not as predictable or as amenable as a piece of machinery. It sleeps late in bed, it can do 'bad work', it can curse the foreman and the boss, it can organise itself, refuse to work, and worse. 'Labour' is the potential source of monumental problems for the corporate bosses. For this reason many plans have been laid in an attempt to deal with it. Those plans take various forms.

The 'small firm sector'

One approach has been concerned, where possible, to minimise the effects of market fluctuations upon the corporation's own workforce. While 'economic necessity' will dictate that certain plants be run down as others are developed, on a day-to-day basis the corporations reckon to benefit from a stable labour force. In Japan, for example, the giant corporations offer their workforces a lifetime of security with the company.[1] This stability, however, is dependant upon the high numbers of *temporary workers* employed by the corporations on low wages and on a hire-and-fire basis. As one account of the Japanese corporation made clear:

> Japan's industrial giants can cushion the blow [of recession] laying off temporary as opposed to 'lifetime' workers and

cutting back on their offtake from thousands of [low wage] medium to pygmy sub-contractors . . .

To those on the lowest rung of the ladder the present almost unreported shake-out will mean very hard times indeed. (*Sunday Times*, 3 March 1974)

In Britain, while not developed to this extent, concerns like the British Steel Corporation and ICI make extensive use of contract labour, particularly for the unpleasant tasks associated with cleaning plant during shut downs. Vickers, and other firms in the engineering industry, regularly *subcontract* work during peak periods. The corporate chiefs are quite clear about the importance to them of this practice. Lord Robens, puts it like this:

If it wasn't for the corporate sector there wouldn't be a small firm; and we'd be in a real mess ourselves if there were no small firms around. We help each other. They're the people who can just take on another chap if they need to produce more of a particular order. Something we would find very difficult to do. They're a very good employment agency, the small firms. They're attached to you like a limpet.

This 'Labour exchange' function has been at the back of the political demands in Britain for support to small firms; something which was made very clear by *The Times*:

Current Department of Employment statistics show that the small firms tend to be non-unionised and to operate more flexible employment policies unimpeded by demarcation criteria, which result in a better strike record . . . They also employ an above national proportion of women and part-time staff. (*The Times*, 22 November 1976)

Subcontracting to such firms can also be used as a threat – we saw the attraction to Vickers of this system at Romford and the closure of the toolroom. In this way a fully developed system of subcontracting from the corporate to the small firm sector would cut the average wages paid to working class people. It would lead to the entrenchment of separate labour markets (one with a high, national wage, the other with significantly lower and locally variable rates) and the possibility of this division being used against workers in each of the sectors. For all these reasons the question of sub-contracting has emerged as a major issue for workers in Vickers, and the various plant committees have been concerned to develop a policy which can regulate it. In many of the larger plants, (e.g. South Marston, Elswick, Crabtree, Leeds), the stewards have won an agreement restricting the company's use of subcontracting. No work is subcontracted unless all of the workers in the plant are fully employed. When subcontracting does take place it is only to fully-unionised plants.

In spite of these agreements there is a feeling amongst combine delegates that a national policy on subcontracting needs to be worked out by shop stewards within Vickers so that work can be shared throughout the company's plants. There is also a feeling that the separateness of the small firm sector and the workers employed in it is a problem which a combine committee structure (based on the corporate sector) cannot adequately deal with by itself.

Living with the unions

Trade unionism is still an issue within the small firm sector; the protracted and defeated strike for union recognition at Grunwick is ample demonstration of this fact. But Grunwick isn't ICI, and George Ward is different indeed from the men who sit on the boards of the giant corporations. These men, in contrast, have learned to live with trade unionism. The experience of the Wilson and Heath governments has shown many employers that direct curtailment of trade union rights is not, in present conditions, a viable strategy. Their alternative is to grant the rights of trade unionism to their workforces and recognise workers representatives – but on the condition that these representatives act responsibly and become 'junior partners' in the corporate enterprise. On a day-to-day basis they *deal* with trade unionism, and are particularly diligent in their attempts to mould trade unionism to fit the corporation's needs.

While 'progressive' employers have for some time realised the advantages to be had from 'bringing the union in', the general acceptance of this as a strategy by the big employers is a comparatively recent phenomenon. It is, for example, only since the war that semi-skilled workers in the USA have established trade union rights. In the USA, and in Britain, many employers still have a rather schizophrenic attitude toward organised workers and their unions: within the rules of the game they are prepared to accept unions and to use what one American labour commentator has termed 'sweet stuff'.[2] Outside of this, though, they are still capable of 'fear stuff' (frightening people about the consequences of joining the union) and, when the rules aren't kept or when 'non-legitimate' claims are made, downright 'evil stuff'. Workers for the big corporations the world over have learned that while the velvet glove may be on show, the iron fist is still inside.

At Vickers, for example, the company spokesman will tell you that the basic principle of the company's industrial relations policy is that 'we recognise the relevant trade union'. However at Slingsby Sailplanes, where the previous, local, businessmen operated anti-union policies, Vickers' takeover brought about no real improvements in the situation of the labour force. While the union is now recognised on the site, its establishment has been fraught with difficulties. On a number of occasions management has escorted union representatives off the site. Stewards say that on several occasions management has refused permission for shop meetings because 'they don't consider them necessary'. While the managers are now forced to concede that they must negotiate on some issues, it's a concession that is given begrudgingly and doesn't go very far.

The workers at KTM in Brighton have had a different (although equally unpleasant) experience of Vickers 'industrial relations policy': KTM is a member of the Engineering Employers Federation and before Vickers' takeover the shop stewards committee had informally established their right to a full-time convenor with an office and telephone extension. This office was used by the four unions at KTM but, with the increased volume of business, the convenor ended up with its full use, the shop stewards of the other unions meeting there occasionally with their members. Management turned a blind eye to this. In joking asides they made reference to the better paid jobs – on the staff and elsewhere – that could be available to a man of the convenor's ability. A joke's a joke – but were they trying to buy him off? He suspected as much but wasn't sure. He felt more certain about management's tactics when he arrived back from his holidays to find that he no longer had access to his office and that he was to be ordered back to his machine. There was, said Vickers management, too much work; but no more than there had been before the holidays or, for that matter, during any of the ten months during which the convenor had been operating full-time. To him, this clamp-down fitted into a trend: 'Since the Vickers takeover the "them and us" division has become more blatant. They only recognise us when it suits them. At first I didn't understand what was going on. But now it fits into a pattern.' At a meeting of the combine committee he asked (half jokingly): 'If you've any more dead wood management in your plants I'd be glad if you'd keep them rather than send them down to us: because you've sent us some beauties I can tell you.'

'Recognition' of the union means many things. And even in the old Vickers' plants, where trade unionism is as old as the machinery itself, the shop stewards have little confidence in the company's formal acceptance of their right to organise. At Scotswood, with the run down of the plant, management announced that the position of full-time convenor was to be withdrawn.

> At least forty years there's been a full time convenor here. At least that. It was up here that all these things originated from . . . places like Elswick were at the beginning of these things . . . We just told them that if they did that they'd have a major dispute on their hands like they'd never seen before.

The decision was withdrawn but seen to be further proof of the Company's underlying approach; an approach which tolerates trade union organisation as an established fact but which insists that it accommodates to managerial rights and authority:

> There's a lot of management in this company who treat shop stewards as if they were there to be given instructions. They came along and demanded that you go to meetings. "I want a meeting with you in half an hour" type of thing . . . We have had to make it clear to a couple of them that if they want a meeting with us – the union — they have to request it and we will consider that request but they can in no way demand that we go to a meeting.

In general, few shop stewards in the company would dispute the assessment of Vickers management which comes from one shop steward in the south: 'At Vickers they don't recognise a trade union, they tolerate it. What I've found with them is that the longer you talk the more the solution moves further away.' And from another in the north:

> We're always on the defensive with management as regards trade unionism because you've still got the archaic management at Vickers who are either anti-trade unionist or think that trade unions are there to be tolerated. You've got them on the floor and you've got them above. We are *always* on the *defensive*.

In the 1950s and early 1960s the Vickers' board was renowned for not dealing with national officers of the trade unions. At that time trade unions were kept at arms length and only dealt with through the Engineering Employers' Federation. The Chairman of Vickers had no inclination to rub shoulders with General Secretaries. By the early 1970s this had certainly changed, and the choice of Robens as chairman is the clearest indication of the new approach. Robens, after all, came up through the system. His life has been built around rubbing shoulders with all sorts, and under his chairmanship the Vickers' boardroom has become much less of an iron cage. Also there is some indication that serious consideration has been given to the 'problem of the unions'. Robens, after his experience as head of the National Coal Board, was particularly unimpressed by the variety of unions and agreements in existence within his new company:

> In this company we have to deal with four separate national agreements. We are forced to conform with the structure of trade unions which have very powerful district committees, following policies which are often different from each other.

It's not that this situation is without advantages – the separation of one plant from another and the fostered ideology of plant independence has served the company well in the past and is still an important force today. It is the basis of the 'fear' tactics (fears promoted about the effect that combine committee membership would have upon wage rates, etc.) used by management against the combine committee in many of the plants. However this policy is in many ways different from the ones being pursued in the major multi-national corporations in Britain. Given the sophisticated and flexible approach to investment planning which these corporations have developed, it makes sense in the context of a unionised labour force to have a corporate plan for labour also. For this reason companies like ICI, Ford, GEC, and Dunlop Pirelli have opted out of their respective employers' federations and set up their own procedures for dealing with disputes and their own national bargaining structures. This represents a systematic attempt to control and regulate the relationship with their labour force. 'Corporate bargaining', as it has been called, represents the giant corporation's most developed and considered response to the problem of union representation and organisation amongst their workforces in Britain. In this attempt they often use the language of the labour movement. For example there was a time when 'industrial unionism' was the militant demand of the syndicalist-inspired shop steward movement in Britain. Today it is the *employers* who are committed to this as an ideal. The President of General Motors, when interviewed on BBC-TV's Panorama programme in July 1974, was in no doubt that industrial unionism was by far the best arrangement for employers: 'There's no question about it – much better, much better.' Union officials make similar reports. A regional official in the north east put it this way,

When I go abroad to encourage employees to come to this area, the first thing they ask is 'How many unions will we have to deal with?' My biggest problem is convincing them that they will not have to negotiate separately with ten to twenty different unions.

In ideal conditions Vickers might prefer a similar – corporate – industrial relations policy. Lord Robens, for example, is strongly committed to the idea of industrial unionism.

The trade union movement in this country was formed in the days of crafts and guilds! It is totally unsuitable to modern conditions. It's like using a penny-farthing bicycle in the jet age. We are reducing the number of unions but what is needed is *industrial unionism*. I am a firm believer in industrial unionism; you only have to look to America to see this.

Ironically, many of the shop stewards who believe in the need for a combine committee also argue the attractions of a company-wide, or industrial structure for their organisation. The reference to 'America' makes clear the difference in emphasis, though. For big business the introduction of company-wide bargaining (and, under pressure, the recognition of some kind of combine committee frame-work) is hedged by the need to keep such bargaining under control. We have already seen that workers can get strength from united action with others who work in different plants of the same company. A fragmented bargaining structure has the advantage (for management) of accentuating splits amongst the workforce. Any recognition of a corporate bargaining entity therefore needs regulation. Thus while shop stewards and the Chairman both talk of 'industrial unionism', Lord Robens is clear that in his company:

> Combine committees mark the road to anarchy. They have no function. They have been set up by power-misers. The plant is where people work and that is where proposed problems should be sorted out. Combine committees will be the ruin of this country. Ford has already moved to Germany and Spain because of bad behaviour at Dagenham . . . And it is this sort of behaviour which has ruined the British ship-building industry.

Vickers has therefore (in its blockade of the road to anarchy) steadfastly refused to recognise the existence of the combine committee or to countenance any discussions or negotiations with its officers. And this opposition has been a major factor in the combine committee's development. It was raised as a problem by one of the shop stewards who attended the meeting at the County Hotel in Newcastle in 1977: 'At the moment', he said, 'the combine huffs and puffs but it doesn't seem to get anywhere with the company. It can't negotiate with the company.' In reply one of the speakers made the situation clear:

> I agree it's a big problem. How do you get the likes of Hendin and Matthews to meet with us? Hendin's quite prepared to come to the north east and meet me but he won't

meet the four of us. He won't sit down with representatives from all the Vickers plants along the Tyne. And the problem isn't just with the company. Vickers is a member of the Federation and its collective bargaining arrangements are within the Confederation.

At Vickers the combine committee structure cuts across the various official negotiating arrangements. This has proven to be a major problem for its recognition by the company. It has also, however, given the committee an important degree of independence from the official trade union structure. It is this which makes it a symbol of 'anarchy'.

However things can change. Several companies, particularly in the car industry, faced the problem of strong, independant combine committees in the 1960s, only to attempt to 'integrate' them in the 1970s. One Ford shop steward describes how he saw the problem:

You develop a combine. It's great. You get people together. You get more force together and more thoughts. Better organisation. But companies don't ignore this fact. The company you work for won't ignore the fact that you're getting together, they will also find a way of combatting what you're doing. And Ford's – it seems to me – have thought this out pretty clearly. They realise now that they cannot combat the combine – it got so organised that it could call a national strike like it did in 1977 with every man jack out for ten weeks. They didn't ignore them or try to squash them because that couldn't be done. It seems to me that what they thought they would do was to try to divorce the convenors and the combine from their fellows. Where there used to be a gulf between the officials and the stewards, they're now developing it where the gulf will be between the convenors and the stewards, and the stewards and the men. They'll spend more time in London than they will be in their own plants, they'll be making decisions themselves . . . and this is what the company is reckoning on: 'We'll have them in and then we'll have control of them because it's harder inside to invent things than it is outside!'

There is nothing inevitable about this. What *is* inevitable however is that big business will *always* attempt to counteract any important degree of independence achieved by workers. In such a strategic game the corporations are extremely flexible in the kinds of structures which they can develop – and still permit the extraction of profit.[3] To recognise this is to appreciate that companies like Vickers could well – in the future – attempt to adapt their collective bargaining arrangements in a way that takes in – and 'institutionalises' – rank-and-file combine committees. Such a policy would certainly be supported by other trends within big business and the British state.

Participation and involvement

'The unions' are but one part of the corporate labour strategy. At plant level the concern has also been with the problem of 'motivation'. Ensuring that workers work hard and attentively has, of course, been a perennial problem for businessmen. In this present, corporate phase, however, the 'problem' has reappeared in an intensified form. The corporations are situated in the most capital-intensive sectors of modern industry. For them it is important that when their plants run, they do so for long periods and at the fullest possible capacity. Absenteeism, lateness, wildcat strikes, shoddy work – the responses of the machine-minders to the wonders of the new technology – are all irritants to the smooth running of the business machine. An official report in the United States noted the feeling of employers that: 'Absenteeism, wildcat strikes, turnover and industrial sabotage have become an increasingly significant part of the cost of doing business.'[4] In an attempt to control such costs, the corporations and national governments have invested large amounts of resources into the study of 'worker motivation'. In Britain the Economic League (an organisation not renowned for its progressive views) has come around to the view that it is important: 'to spread at board room level information concerned with motivation and the help which can come from the behavioural sciences on matters of industrial conduct.'[5]

In this context, firms like ICI have been in the vanguard of developing schemes for the involvement of workers in the corporation and the 'enrichment' of their (deskilled) work, while Lonrho, on taking over Brentford Nylons, declared itself committed to 'revolutionary capitalism', based around establishing 'the vital bond between managers and workers without which no business can function' (*Sunday Times*, 15 August 1976).

'Participation', 'consultation', 'human relations', are all grist to this particular mill. The mushrooming of consultation and participation schemes reflects this 'revolution', and the policies of the Labour government elected in 1974 have strengthened the tendency towards employee participation in management. This policy is particularly likely to speed the establishment of company-wide employee 'participation' schemes in companies which have not, so far, developed corporate negotiating structures. One example of this tendency was to be seen in the Labour government's *White Paper on Industrial Democracy*. This argued for the setting up of bodies very similar to combine committees, a fact that was noted in *Shop Floor Voice*, which reproduced an extract from the White Paper under the headline 'Combine democracy Becomes Respectable':

How should the rights to discussion operate in groups of companies and multinationals? In groups of companies it will therefore be necessary for discussions to take place between representatives of employees and companies both at subsidiary and holding company levels, and perhaps at intermediate company levels too, depending upon where decisions are taken. Where a JRC (combine shop stewards' committee) is formed at group level by independent recognised unions in the group it should have the right to discussions with the parent company on any major proposals made at that level affecting the business of the group as a whole or of any of the subsidiary companies.

The forms of corporate participation which are eventually proposed, let alone practised, are unlikely to be as specific, or so directly based on shop stewards organisation. However it seems likely that in multi-industry companies such as Vickers, this 'consultative route' to company-wide dealings with unions is the most likely avenue for management to explore. It is already becoming clear that the function of these schemes is to draw workers into discussion – not negotiations – within a framework set by management. Discussion takes place, but on management's terms – terms which *justify* rationalisations and job-saving investments.

Too often convenors and shop stewards who work with such schemes find that they get caught up in innumerable joint committees, and sometimes even in carrying out the 'progress-chasing' function of management. ICI operate such a scheme, and one shop steward on their Wilton site described his experience of it in this way:

> I've given the investment committee two years and I'm thinking seriously about resigning. The consultation we're involved in is no more than we could get from a careful reading in the *Financial Times*. It's a question of them telling us what the future plans are: once the decisions have been made. The only advance information I get is always 'in confidence'. I'm never told anything that I can use to benefit my members.

At Chrysler, shop stewards had a similar experience. On 6 October 1977 the shop floor representatives on the management-trade union working party at the Ryton factory asked for information about the future production plans for the new light car (the Tango). Management had threatened to move Tango production from Linwood to Ryton and the stewards saw this as pressure upon the Linwood workforce aimed at getting a flexibility agreement accepted in the plant. In these circumstances the Ryton shop stewards were keen to get more information on the details of the case. However, information was not forthcoming. In fact the working party – which came into existence to draw up the company's long awaited planning agreement – was adjourned (see *Financial Times*, 30 December 1977), not to be reconvened for six months. By that time 'flexibility' had been agreed at Linwood.

At Vickers the company declares that its 'firm policy' is:

> that there should be the fullest possible flow of information to all employees, that there should be machinery for regular consultation in each constituent business of the Group, and that there should be a clear path for any employee to achieve Board membership.

In its submission to the Committee of Inquiry on Industrial Democracy (the Bullock Committee) the company claimed that such procedures had been used to arrive at the 'company's view':

VICKERS

A Proposal for Worker Involvement

in Management

"I see it as the role of Government, and of the Organising Committee, and the Board and the Unions themselves, to stimulate and encourage and support moves by workers in industry to hammer out their own proposals for the structure of the Industry and the injection of a genuinely democratic element into the management pattern." Mr Tony Benn, addressing a conference in Gateshead on 24 March 1975 on the subject of the Labour Party's policies on Industry.

The Vickers North East Shop Stewards Committees, anticipating the thinking of the Minister on this issue, set up the working party at the beginning of 1975. Its broad terms of reference were to examine and analyse the existing management control structure and to draw up alternative democratic structures. After looking at the present structure, we came to the following major conclusions:

 (1) There is already a large element of control of the working environment at shop floor level by shop stewards and members, in negotiation,discussion and sometimes through industrial action.

 (2) However, as workers we do not have a voice on the boards where, in the main, the decisions are made that we have to work to on the shop floor.

Our proposal, then, is simply 50% worker representation on the boards, at Local or plant level, (where they exist), at Group product level and at National level. This proposal is broadly in line with the TUC policy (as outlined in the statement on 'Industrial Democracy') for 50% membership of boards to be elected through the Trade Union machinery where more than 2000 workers are employed in a company. We do feel, however, that one of the primary matters that the new boards should deal with is to make management structures more responsive and more democratic.

Our ideas assume that Vickers will be subject to Labour Party and TUC industrial policies, and to the current Industry Legislation proposals. The document has been widely circulated at shop floor level and comments welcomed. In addition to discussions at the North East works, the document has been discussed by the Vickers Combine Committee. The only qualification expressed by some shop stewards is that worker directors on the various boards should be allowed to remain shop stewards.

The Working Group Members were: Peter Tolchard (Scotswood Works - Chairman), Tom Odell (Crabtree-Vickers, Gateshead), Robin Gray (Michell Bearings), Jim Murray (Elswick Works), with the involvement of the Benwell Community Project.

The views expressed in this submission take the form of a resume of opinions by a selection of employees at various levels, conferences and discussions over the period in which the subject has been widely debated within the company.

This was news to the combine committee. It was particularly irritating too, as three years earlier they had produced their own proposals for a very different sort of 'participation' in the company (see page 173). In this they called for 50-50 worker/management representation on all the company's major decision-making bodies. The company agreed to discuss these proposals 'at the appropriate moment'. That moment has still to arrive. Clearly such a scheme has no chance of being accepted willingly by big business, and the combine committee is aware that any compromise around such proposals could be turned to the company's advantage. It is for this reason that they (and other committees throughout the corporate sector) have been concerned to discuss and work out a more elaborate counter-strategy, one which moves beyond the limits imposed by the company structure. As the present economic recession continues, and as the consequences of management's policies unfold, such an alternative becomes a matter of urgency.

Chapter 14

An Alternative Future?

Fifty years ago G. D. H. Cole, the theoretician of the British guild socialist tradition, reflected upon the militant factory-based struggles which he had been involved in around the time of the first world war. These struggles – built around the 'first shop stewards movement' – ended in failure as economic recession preceded the great lock-out of 1926. This collapse, wrote Cole, had much to do with the movement's failure to shift its attention from the shop floor and toward 'the higher reaches of control . . . especially the control over investment'.[1] While the parallels between now and then are rather complex, this one observation retains its force, for this particular vulnerability of shop floor organisation to the flexibility of capital is heightened in the modern context. Recognition of this has led shop stewards committees and their combine organisations to question the established limits of their relationship with the companies. The combine committees at Lucas Aerospace, Rolls Royce, ICI, and the power supply industry have all discussed the question of developing workers' plans for investment, an idea which has been strongly supported by shop stewards within Vickers Ltd. A shop steward at Hastie Brothers on Clydeside put it like this:

> I think it is crucial that we should know of their investment
> plans and have alternative plans of our own to fight for. We
> need to be much more prepared for their decisions. At the
> moment we just react, and its usually too late. I think we
> should be hammering for alternative plans at every outlet
> available. It has to be the combine committee that will force
> our national executive into demanding them!

Views like this one provide the basis of a strategy for labour which can combat that being developed by the corporations and the government. This final chapter of the *Workers' Report* outlines the development of this strategy and examines its relevance to the Vickers combine committee and the workers it represents.

The 'boom' collapses

The 1960s were boom years during which militant bargaining on the shop floor enabled many sections of the working class to advance their living standards. It was in such conditions that the early combine committees (like the one at BMC) were formed. But the boom – although the longest and most remarkable one in memory – did not last; and the recession has served to emphasise the growing vulnerability of British companies in the global market place. The 1970s have as a result (and in stark contrast to the earlier decade) been years when redundancy, plant closure and rationalisation have emerged as the main problems faced by workers and their organisations. We have seen how this operated in the case of Vickers, and how it was presented to the workers as an inevitable law, a consequence of 'the hard facts of economic life'. Generally, these 'facts' have been enforced by statutory wage controls and arguments which stressed the common interests we all have in solving the crisis. In these circumstances attempts to regain lost bargaining strength, to resist the controls, and talk of 'free collective bargaining' and of the need to fight closures, have been met with argument about profitability, inflation, the nature of 'the crisis', the constraints of the market, and so on.

A system that works tolerably well and manages to satisfy many of the needs of the people can avoid such self-examination; its members are generally spared the exhortations of people at the top, justifying things and demanding more commitment, more sacrifice. An economic crisis, however – particularly one which spills millions of people out of work – makes ideological and political debate inevitable. For those on the receiving end, those who make the sacrifices, the logic of a system which doesn't work is difficult to accept. Mike Cooley of the Lucas Aerospace combine committee put it like this:

We have a level of technological sophistication such that we can design and produce Concorde, yet in the same society we cannot provide enough simple heating systems to protect old age pensioners from hypothermia. In the winter of 1975–76, 980 died of the cold in the London area alone . . .

Added to this is: the tragic wastage [which] our society makes of its most precious asset – that is the skill, ingenuity, energy, creativity and enthusiasm of its ordinary people. We now have in Britain 1.6 million people out of work. There are thousands of engineers suffering the degradation of the dole queue when we urgently need cheap, effective and safe transport systems for our cities. There are thousands of electricians robbed by society of the right to work when we urgently need economic urban heating systems. We have I believe, 180,000 building workers out of a job when by the government's own statistics it is admitted that about 7 million people live in semi-slums in this country. In the London area we have about 20 per cent of the schools without an indoor toilet, when the people who could be making these things are rotting away in the dole queue.[2]

Given all this it is perhaps surprising that things have been as quiet as they have been; that there haven't been more strikes, more factory occupations, more marches in London. Perhaps the surprising thing is the extent to which redundancy (via the provisions of the Redundancy Payments Act) has been accepted by so many workers and their organisations. Many things are involved here. But one of them is surely that working class people, while recognising these contradictions and agreeing that much in our society is not as it should be (if not completely around the bend), feel powerless to do anything about it. They can see no alternative. For example in January, 1975 Panorama ran a programme based on the crisis facing Chrysler's operations in Britain. David Dimbleby talked with a group of car workers in a pub in Coventry. During the discussion they revealed a deep antipathy toward the company and the way they had been treated. In his final penetrating question Dimbleby asked, 'How do you save jobs if you can't sell the cars?' The reply came slowly: 'That's a good question which I cannot answer.'

The combine committee at Vickers is determined to come up with an answer. The shop stewards there have come to realise –

North unions fight for worker control

By PAUL NUNN, Industrial Reporter

POWERFUL trade union pressure groups from the North-East's biggest firms are joining forces to fight for worker control.

Leading shop stewards from companies like Vickers, Swan Hunters, Reyrolle Parsons, Alcan, Clarke Chapman, Courtaulds, Tube Investments and Scottish and Newcastle are to form an action group.

They will study Mr. Tony Benn's controversial Industry Bill and are likely to push for changes in it before it becomes law.

Most of them feel that the companies to be nationalised and those who will be subject to "planning agreements" will still not be subject to enough worker control, unless the bill is improved.

The movement is particularly strong at Vickers.

through their experience of run-down and many long discussions – that the corporate economy is not going to provide them and their children with a secure future. To quote one of them:

> That's what I'm doing all this for. Not necessarily for me but for my children and my grandchildren. It's important that we provide some sort of future for them; a future that is better than what we've had. As far as I can see at the moment there's going to be no future at all – because there's going to be no bloody jobs. That's how I look at it.

In building their combine organisation, and arguing over its tactics and strategies, they have established the principle that all struggles over redundancy and plant closure will be supported throughout the company. They have supported such struggles with demands for work-sharing between plants, the resistance to sub-contracting, and 'pressure' upon MPs and local councillors. Increasingly, however, they have expressed the need to go beyond these activities, to fight against the very structure of the corporation and the economy of which it is a part. For while traditional trade union demands proved effective at Scotswood on Tyneside in 1977, and there can be little doubt that an organised combine committee would have been of great assistance in the fight to save Water Lane, these traditional demands do have their limits. At Water Lane, the recession in the printing machinery industry had placed the plant in a particularly vulnerable position. In terms of the logic of profit and loss the argument for closure was a powerful one. So powerful that it exerted a demoralising effect upon the workforce. To combat the closure would have required organis-ational muscle (the weapon, if you like) and the determination to use it. Such determination is built upon many things, but one of them is *argument*. In struggle you need something to fight for, you also need to feel that you can win, that you have the right to win and that the victory will be a lasting one. With the collapse of the boom, shop stewards committees throughout British industry find that they are often, perhaps unintentionally, challenging more than their particular management. Increasingly they find themselves in arguments which involve questioning, to differing degrees, the market as an adequate measure of need, the necessity of investment decisions based on profit criteria, and the constraints of the government and of the financial institutions. In many respects their discussions touch upon the need for an *alternative* future.

The old way forward

Historically, British trade unions have relied upon their alliance with the Labour Party (the two making up the so-called 'industrial' and 'political' wings of the labour movement) to solve the problem of an alternative strategy through parliamentary action. During the 1930s – the last major economic crisis in Britain – the search for a means of organising production to meet the social needs of the people focused on a programme for the nationalisation of the major industries. Political control over the state machine would allow the Labour Party to take the major industries into social ownership. From this commanding position, production could be planned according to the needs of working people, either as workers or as consumers. However things haven't worked out quite like this.

One man, who now works for Vickers at Elswick and used to be a pitman, remembers the high expectations of the mining communities:

I can remember standing at the pit with the banners, celebrating with my father and his friends. They thought, this was it. What a surprise they were going to get. They thought nationalisation would bring everything they'd fought for. But within a very short space of time they found out that they'd swapped one boss for another. The first boss we got under nationalisation was a major from the Indian Army, six months later followed by a Captain Nicholson . . . later we had a banker!

A shop steward at South Marston worked on the railways and was similarly disillusioned:

We really believed it would make a difference. We really thought it was the beginning of socialism, you know, almost time to hoist the red flag. I thought we'd be working for ourselves, that we'd be in control. But in fact the supervision and bureaucratic administration became a hundred times worse. You'd get 10 foremen where before you only had one; you'd have to use 10 pieces of paper where before you'd only have one. You'd always have to go through many more channels to get anything done. That approach killed nationalisation. A lot of us felt really frustrated. Mind, I still think nationalisation is the only way, but next time it will have to be very different.

Looking back, many activists in the combine committee at Vickers now see that these experiences are not altogether surprising. Nationalisation has produced no real alteration in the balance of power within the work place or in society as a whole; neither has it altered the dominant logic which governs the 'success' and 'failure' of a particular company. Nationalisation has not affected the dominant logic of profit; if anything it has been the basis for sustaining that logic within British industry generally. Vickers, a medium sized corporation (operating still with the government as its major market), has managed to call all the shots in its dealings with the British state. For people on the shop floor it seems that the Labour cabinet and parliamentary party are pretty much the prisoners – often willingly so – of the existing relations of industrial and social power.[3] This disillusionment, heightened during the last years of the Wilson government, fostered the feeling during the early 1970s that Clause Four was not enough; new policies would have to be tried.

During the years of opposition a 'new strategy' was developed within the Labour Party which gave form to the manifesto with which it fought the 1974 general election. It consisted of proposals to nationalise key companies in each manufacturing sector in order, from this base, to set standards of 'social responsibility' for the other companies to follow. This would be backed up by making 'planning agreements' with the remaining companies, thereby bringing them into line with social priorities. Establishment of a National Enterprise Board which would give financial assistance and establish public enterprises according to these priorities was also foreseen.

Labour Party leaders like Tony Benn, helped by the Institute for Workers Control, argued the need to back their proposals with detailed contacts with the shop stewards committees in the corporate sector who had a direct interest in the proposals and the industrial strength to exert pressure in support of them. The shop stewards of the Vickers combine committee were involved in those contacts and on Tyneside they initiated the Tyne Shop Stewards Conference as part of an attempt to build a rank-and-file alliance. This conference (which attracted over eighty representatives from shop stewards committees in the multinational corporations on Tyneside) organised regular monthly meetings based around the specific policies outlined in the 1973 Labour Party Manifesto. At these meetings workers expressed the feelings that the policies could provide a basis for a strategy to control the power of the corporations.

All this, however, came to nothing. The proposals outlined in the manifesto never got off the ground. Benn was shifted out of the Department of Industry, the Industry Bill was emasculated and planning agreements were made voluntary. The NEB was transformed into an instrument for carrying out rationalisations which private capital did not have the strength to impose. As the *Guardian* put it in 1976, commenting on the NEB's final statutory guidelines, 'the lion's teeth are well and truly drawn'. With this the Tyneside Conference lost its impetus. It was to be the same as before. The 'social contract' reaffirmed the old industrial and political alliance of the labour movement. The policies of Tony Benn and the new Labour left foundered on rocks which had an all too familiar look about them.

Workers' plans: a new departure?

For all the problems and weaknesses of the 1973 proposals they did represent an attempt to deal with the question of corporate power in a recession. Their failure simply emphasised to many people the need for strategies which could go beyond the traditional separation of 'trade union' and 'political' action. Those combine committees (like Vickers and Lucas) who had had close contact with the Labour Party's proposals were thrown back on their own resources. They were left with the feeling that they would need to develop plans of their own, organised 'from below'. It is in this context that there has been discussion (within the corporate sector particularly) of the idea of *workers'* plans and alternative production.

The alternative corporate plan drawn up by Lucas Aerospace shop stewards combine committee is probably the best known of these developments. It was produced initially in the period of the 'rank-and-file' alliance as a response to problems which were similar, in some respects, to those facing workers in Vickers. Lucas Aerospace had followed a policy of rationalisation which had seen the reduction of the workforce from 18,000 in 1970 to 13,000 in 1974, with the prospect of further cuts to come. At the same time the company was producing, in very small numbers and at extremely high prices, kidney machines for which (if the number of pub collections is anything to go by) there was and is an urgent need. This contradiction appeared as a glaring one to the Lucas committee: the plant and the workforce exist – why not stop the sackings and make more kidney machines? The 'alternative' plan grew out of this. It was this which led the Lucas workers to go beyond demanding 'the right to work' and to argue for a plan which demonstrated that products – for which there was a real, social need – could be produced in the Lucas plants. In moving in this direction the Lucas workers raised issues of fundamental political importance.

Initially there was the question of *social usefulness*: by what criteria do we, in this society, decide upon what is to be produced? This was raised quite dramatically in a company which produced a few kidney machines but massive amounts of equipment for warfare, and raised the further question of how technological advance is related to human needs. At Lucas, for example, the company had developed sophisticated aids to allow pilots to land 'blind' – aids which contrast graphically with the white sticks blind people rely upon. Many other examples came to mind. The combine committee became particularly interested in the possibility of developing a hybrid electric-petrol vehicle which would reduce fuel consumption and pollution, and also a light-weight rubber-wheeled vehicle, capable of running on roads or rails. Two products whose potential had never been fully developed by Lucas company.

In our society the market determines what is produced. And it is the market-place which has always provided the main source of justification for capitalism. The market, it is argued, satisfies people's needs, it offers choice, it ensures that goods are only produced if they are wanted and thereby makes the closure of plants producing 'unwanted' lines inevitable. But one of the real problems of the market lies in the fact that only certain 'demands' are registered. 'Demand' depends upon 'money' and in a society where money is distributed extremely unequally, the market reflects this distortion. This has always been the case.

Under the monopoly control of the corporation, however, other distortions have emerged. As the companies developed the techniques of mass production they realised that once people obtained what they needed cheaply, markets became saturated. So the markets were regulated: new 'brands' were established and 'saturation' was avoided by built-in obsolescence and the yearly round of the 'new model'. Today 'competition on the High Street' usually involves a choice between a range of similarly priced brands of similar quality. Often these commodities are produced by two or three mammoth companies, and it is not exceptional for 'competition' to be between the brands of the same company. Unilever, for example, produces over a thousand products, in seven main manufacturing areas. It hardly ever trades under the name of 'Unilever' yet hundreds of brands which have become household names (Lux, Persil, Omo, Vim, Harmony, Close-up, Signal, Blue Band, Stork, Crisp n' Dry, Birds Eye, Vesta, Walls, Unox, etc., etc.) – are produced in factories which it owns.

The monopoly power exercised by the corporations also gives them control over advanced technology, its form, the way it is introduced and the products which it produces. And this has consequences *inside* the factory as well as in the market place. We saw in part three of this report that technological development is a 'management function' and that management is in a position to develop techniques which will secure – or extend – its control over the factory floor: deskilling of work and the routinisation of the work process are clear examples of this. The Lucas committee drew attention to this and made it clear that their plan for the company extended well beyond a 'suggestion scheme' for alternative products: it was a plan which asked fundamental questions about 'corporate planning' and the nature of an alternative way of organising society. Its fundamental strength was that it showed in practical terms that *there is no need for redundancies*; there are real social needs which now unnecessarily go unmet, because people and machinery that are considered redundant could, if things were organised differently, meet those needs.

At Vickers, the combine committee has also accepted the importance of developing workers' planning. They found the experience of the Lucas workers familiar enough and they see the relevance of this initiative to their situation. However they are also aware of some differences between Vickers and Lucas.

Perhaps the biggest difference has to do with Vickers' position as a multi-industry corporation. The company still makes armaments but it also produces medical equipment and office furniture. As one shop steward put it, 'Vickers kills them, heals them and files them'. A 'social usefulness' of a sort! Practically it means that, in the Vickers situation, the question of 'socially useful production' and its role as the basis for workers' planning appears in a more complicated form than it does at Lucas Aerospace. Furthermore, the Lucas Aerospace combine committee includes a large number of technical and white collar workers – for the most part members of TASS (the AUEW white collar group). We have seen that the Vickers combine committee is quite different in this respect. Within most of Vickers' production plants, there are very few technical workers. The company's technical labour force is concentrated within certain divisions which have not been affected deeply by rationalisation. As a result the combine committee at Vickers argues that the 'Lucas Plan' cannot be taken as a blue print, that it is impossible, and not necessarily desirable, for them to produce a single 'corporate plan' for the company. Neither need their emphasis be on *alternative* products, except perhaps at Elswick. At their meetings they have given thought to just what might be possible, and this has come up in a variety of ways.

Initially the question of armaments production at Elswick was extremely important. Many of the people who worked in the plant were not too happy with using their skills to produce instruments of destruction, and the works committee strongly supported moves within the Labour Party to cut defence expenditure. For the committee the cuts were seen to be important both in terms of national priorities and the situation in the plant. The 'old Vickers' was built on armaments, on 'the service element' and a curious *cameraderie* of warfare. The committee would happily see the end of all that. The question however was 'what else will we produce?' Ideals are well enough but people need jobs. In this context the Elswick shop stewards co-operated with members of the National Executive of the Labour Party in examining the possibility of a planned conversion of 'defence capacity' into 'socially useful production'. At Elswick they examined the human skills and resources that went into the production of the Chieftain Tank and suggested how those same skills and resources could be put to alternative use. They discussed the possibility of producing heat pumps, recycling plant and oil-spillage pumps; they have also talked of small brewing machinery and the possibility of making agricultural equipment for the third world.[4]

The investigation at Elswick has not developed to the level of a workers plan for Vickers, or even for the Elswick factory. What it has done – in the context of all the other waste that has accompanied Vickers modernisation – is to suggest that there is an alternative way. It suggests that decisions over what can and need to be produced are ones which workers could control, if it were not for the way production is at present organised; that these decisions on 'what is produced', on 'which plants stay open and which close', can be seen as practical questions outside of the accounting framework of profit and loss which dominates corporate decision making. This, taking place at the same time as the Lucas proposals, and at a time when the need to challenge management plans has become so urgent, has helped to stimulate a wider interest in the idea of workers' plans. Within Vickers itself the initiative gained strength with the compensation money paid to the Company as a result of the nationalisation of the shipbuilding and aerospace industries. This money (which could equal the value of Vickers' present assets) raised the issue of control particularly starkly. Amid much speculation in the financial press, it was the view of Sir Peter Matthews – the man at the top – that was avidly sought by reporters. He announced that any decision taken about use of this money would be based upon the interests of the shareholders – after all it is their company. But to many of the people who work for Vickers the right of shareholders to control the compensation money (let alone the right to keep it for themselves!) was questionable. They may *own* the company through their wealth and their purchase of shares but that doesn't make it theirs! Don't the

men and women who work the machines have any rights in all this? Didn't they have a hand in the production of all the wealth which made Vickers?[5]

The last time Vickers received a dose of 'compensation' it was followed by run-down, take-overs and closures. Next time, people argue, it must be different. But how? Within the Vickers' combine committee (and within rank-and-file committees generally) there is disagreement over the extent to which workers and their representatives should actively involve themselves in questions of investment. Some people feel that they have not the expertise, that these complex decisions are best left to 'the brains' at the top. Others fear that the extension of trade union militancy beyond the traditionally accepted limits of collective bargaining will simply involve unionists in the business of management and succeed only in integrating them into management's system. While these latter fears are not groundless, they apply more to involvement in participation schemes than to the extension of collective bargaining – the extension of the issues which are subject to negotiations and industrial action. The extension of collective bargaining does not threaten the independence of workers organisations in the way that involvement in participation schemes can. At Vickers, the majority view within the combine committee is that these matters need to be tackled head on, and that the issue of the compensation money offers the focus for a campaign around the whole purpose of investment and the right of working class people to control their own lives. This campaign (at the time of writing) is in its formative stage. It aims to base itself on ideas for and from each plant and locality involved in the Vickers empire, asking workers to examine where there has been a lack of investment, where people are unemployed who could work at their plant, where there are needs which their plant could meet. On Tyneside the North East Working Party is considering plans for expanding the Scotswood plant, reversing the run-down of both the plant and of Tyneside and providing jobs for the thousands of workers made redundant by the decline of engineering and shipbuilding in the area. Their discussions have touched on the construction of hydrofoils for use as a rapid transport service along the Tyne, heat pumps, solar panels, large-scale tracked vehicles for the construction industry, and a number of other products. The discussions in the Crabtree plant in Gateshead have produced criticism of the company's take-over policy, especially of the kind of rationalisations that have resulted. They have talked, too, of a shorter working week and improved conditions of work.

In these ways the question of 'production for profit or for use?' is being raised once again within the British working class. At present (within Vickers and generally) such 'workers' plans' have not been developed very far. However in the *possibility* they present of things being organised differently (of different things being produced, at different prices, under different conditions) they appear as a powerful ideological weapon for workers in struggle. In substance the plans represent a demand for *workers control over production*. As a final point in this report we need to ask about the problems facing such a demand? How realistic are campaigns for workers' plans as a strategy in the present situation? What new forms of organisation are necessary for their development?

Who will support workers' plans?

Trade unionism has gone some way to assert the human needs of the worker. But it has tended to do this mainly within the limits of the wage contract: bargaining over wages and conditions, while taking the purpose of production, the technology, and employers control over investment as given. Workers' plans place a question mark over all of these assumptions. In drawing up such plans workers have to look critically at the organisation of the markets, the priorities of investment, the division of labour, the use of automation, the social effects of machine tool designs etc.

If this is what workers' plans involve you might be excused for thinking them an impossibility. Certainly a number of strong objections could be made. To begin with, will people be interested? Workers' plans may be useful as a tactic specific to groups of highly skilled workers with a commitment to the technicalities of their job, but how relevant are they to the lives of semi-skilled assembly workers like those who work on the assembly line at Roneo Vickers? Most of the people who endure the monotony of assembly line work dislike their jobs and feel little or no commitment to their work. Given half a chance they'd prefer to be somewhere else. How can they be expected to show any interest in plans to re-organise production in order to save their jobs?

These are fair points and several things follow from them. For one, it is clear that workers' plans must take a serious interest in the division of labour and in the kind of jobs that are being produced in the modern factories. The 'quality of life' in the factory should be a central feature of a workers' plan. Having said this, though, it mustn't be forgotten that semi-skilled workers have experienced the sequence of rationalisation with an intensity equal to (if not in excess of) that experienced by skilled workers. Throughout the country, light engineering factories (the 'boom industries' of the 1960s) have closed. Works committees in some of these factories have taken up the issues of alternative production: belatedly the idea of alternative products (a car with the hybrid engine produced in tandem with Lucas Aerospace) was raised in connection with the closure of Leyland's plant at Speke. As one man put it, 'I don't think we should be producing bleeding sports cars that nobody can afford anyway. That plant could produce something useful'.[6]

In a similar situation the shop stewards committee at Massey Ferguson floated the idea of producing tractors – under a state subsidy – for underdeveloped countries. The fact is that as plant closures increase in frequency, alternative possibilities are being raised quite generally.

This leads to a further point, arising from the nature of the present economic crisis. The present recession, while at the moment less intense, is a much more general and permanent phenomenon than that experienced in the 1930s. There are few jobs that workers can come by through migrating south or (for the Welsh) east. Rationalisation and technical change has produced a kind of unemployment which is more structural than cyclical, with little hope of closed plants opening again in a year or so 'when we've weathered the storm'. The workforce is different too. It is generally more strongly organised into trade unions. People's expectations were built up in the boom years, unaffected by war and conscription, and accepting welfare (to an extent) as a right. Given a lead these people might well respond to new, bold and imaginative attempts to alter things. But this is speculation. It has to be tested.

A question of ownership

The new departure suggested by workers' planning differs most markedly from previously tried strategies in that 'public owner- ship' has not appeared as an immediate objective. The old logic rested on the assumption that the exproportion of private capital (through 'state ownership') was sufficient to challenge the logic of profit. The logic which led Ford to produce the Pinto, the logic which, in the past, lead Vickers to sell arms to anyone who will buy – to both sides if possible! – is the logic of a capitalist economy. The fight for alternative, social plans will continually clash with this logic. In so far as workers are successful in extending collective bargaining and exerting pressure to affect investment decisions against the wishes of capital then it is to be expected that private capital (especially the giant corporations and financial institutions) will take action in reply – political pressure, the movement of funds, the threat of 'economic collapse', leading articles in the *Mail* and the *Sun*. The pattern is a familiar one. In this way, in the context of the corporate economy, the issue of ownership cannot be avoided.[7]

The people who talk about workers' plans and who are attempt- ing to develop them accept the importance of ownership. What they are wary of, though, is the prospect of exchanging one form of ownership (the private employer) for another (the state). The British workers' experience of the state as an employer has been a chastening one. Workers' plans seem to offer the prospect of certain short-term gains – particularly for workers facing redundancy. Furthermore organising for the 'alternative plan' in itself could strengthen the workers organisations and provide a basis for a different kind of public ownership. In this perspective the question of ownership would be seen as not so much an end in itself as a necessary condition for the implementation of plans and priorities that were *already being fought for*.

So how, in the context of a capitalist economy, can workers' plans be formulated and organised for? What part can they play in the day- to-day struggle with the employer in the factory? And what relevance do they have to those members of the working class who do not work in factories or within the corporate sector?

Organising for workers' plans

The idea of workers' planning has come out of shop stewards' organisations and they have been argued for most clearly through combine committees. As such workers planning has tended to focus upon *the company* as a basis for re-organising production. And this creates a problem. Given the way corporations like Vickers have developed it is unlikely that they will provide the most satisfactory context for workers' plans. Also, within the confines of the company, the committees are likely to come up against attempts by management to convert alternative planning into 'participation' and 'suggestion schemes'. If such plans are to develop their potential the workers' organisations will need to go beyond the factory and the company. And there are signs that such developments are taking place.

At Vickers the combine committee has attempted to set up links with committees in other companies, aimed at establishing a regional and national shop steward framework within the corporate sector. At Lucas, the combine committee found that in order to establish some priority as to 'social need' and 'social usefulness' they had to discuss production problems with people other than Lucas workers. In Burnley, for example, ideas for the alternative plan have been discussed in detail with representatives from the trades council, community groups and other local trade union bodies. Some of the combine committee's proposals for economical and non-polluting heating systems have stimulated links with community and environmental groups.

Already it is clear that the kind of linkages which are necessary if workers are to develop their own plan will vary enormously. In some cases – e.g. some aspects of office equipment or the food industry – the development of alternative plans might only involve contact between local industrial workers' organisations and local service sector and community organisations. In others national (and ultimately international) links within an industry, and with the workers in the user industries, would be necessary. The fight for the production of kidney machines at Lucas makes contact with workers in the National Health Service essential. At Vickers, too, any re-organisation of production (give the presence of the government as the company's major customer) would inevitably involve workers in the state sector. While much of this could develop in an *ad hoc* manner it is clear that workers' planning will not be conceded without an important degree of co-ordinated industrial and political pressure. And this will need to be organised too.

Over the last four years the bare bones of such a network of contact has been built up on a local and national level. The combine committees (for all their difficulties and imperfections) mark an important development themselves. Within particular industries this contact has been extended. The machine tool industry (in which Vickers is represented through KTM) provides particularly favourable conditions for such contacts. It is relatively compact – seven companies control nearly 50 per cent of output – and the workers within it are highly skilled – jobs are often passed down from father to son – and have an established tradition of strong shop floor organisation. Afraid of the effects that Japanese imports would have upon employment, shop stewards (along with research workers from the Coventry workshop) made a detailed study of their industry and concluded that imports were not the primary threat. The real problem was that the owners had been investing a relatively small proportion of the profits they had made from the industry over the years. As a result the shop committees focused their attention on control of investment, and the problems involved in planning the industry and its relation to the people who use the machine tools. The contacts have thus been made for an industry-wide combine in machine tools and this has been extended through contacts with workers in the car industry.

While these developments have been taking place in factories, in the community and within the service sector, grass roots organisations have also been established. These have fought social expenditure cuts and the general deterioration of housing and community facilities. They have been concerned to demand increased facilities in the community, especially for children and women. These organisations are therefore also challenging the priorities of capitalist planning, albeit defensively. Usually, however, they are weakened by the lack of an organised relationship with workers in the manufacturing and construction sectors. There are difficulties in establishing such links, but 'alternative plans' which point to the common interests of public and private sector workers, and to the fact that the crisis is a crisis of *profits*, could help overcome these. Organised links could strengthen the arguments that lead to practical plans being fought for through industrial, community and political action. Such organisation would place a far more effective pressure on corporate and government decision making than the fragmented lobbies and campaigns which exist at present. The idea of 'alternative plans' offers the prospect of a qualitative advance in struggles on all these fronts.

All this, of course, is pretty make-shift, particularly when compared with the detailed analyses of cost and benefit that take place at the corporate centres. But if after the last two centuries or so of capitalist 'rationality' we are still faced with the same saga of crisis and unemployment, maybe a cockeyed solution has some-thing going for it. Capitalism is about production for profit: any joy, happiness, or contentment that's achieved is almost incidental, a by-product of the main process. But cannot a society be organised around the expressed needs of the people who live in it? Can these feelings never figure in decisions about production? In 1938 Jack Common, a novelist and political writer born on Tyneside, wrote of his favourite strike – the time in 1912 when the pease pudding men struck over a workmate sacked for being found drunk one evening on a company-owned bus:

> More than most it is a clue to what power there can be in this method of upsetting the current iniquities. The TUC if it did not consist so largely of hardened old bargainers might delight us all if only it would call stoppages in favour of more general amenities. It could make England a gayer land for us all. The material is there, amply, but not the imagination.

The prospect of workers' planning is one which builds on the material; builds on it with imagination, providing the basis for a saner (and ultimately more rational) way of organising society.

References

Chapter 1
The Corporate Economy

[1]
General information about the corporate sector can be obtained from
S Holland, *The Socialist Challenge*, London Quartet 1976; and S J Prais,
The Evolution of Giant Firms in Britain, Cambridge University Press
1976. For information relating to the Corporations on Tyneside see
The costs of Industrial Change, Benwell Community Development
Project 1974 (84 Adelaide Terrace, Benwell, Newcastle); for
Merseyside see *Manufacturing Industry in the Inner City; a case study of
Merseyside*, North West Industry Research Unit, University of
Manchester 1977.

[2]
M Z Brooke and H L Remmers, *The Strategy of the
Multinational Enterprise*, Cambridge, Mass., MIT Press 1970.

[3]
A Sampson, *The Sovereign state: The Secret History of ITT*, London,
Hodder and Stoughton 1973, p. 119.

[4]
R J Barnet and R E Muller, *Global Reach*, New York, Simon &
Schuster 1974, p. 36.

[5]
Originally reported in an article by Mark Davie, 'Pinto madness',
published in an American journal, *Mother Jones*, September/October
1977, and reprinted in the *Counter Information Service Report on Ford*,
London, CIS 1978.

The internal memorandum was reported in *The Sunday Times*, 12
December 1978, after a US jury had awarded Richard Grimshaw – one
of the burn victims – $128 million in compensation and punitive
damages.

[6]
Barnet and Muller, *op.cit.*, p. 41.

[7]
Quoted in M Foot, *Aneurin Bevan, 1897–1945*, London, MacGibbon & Kee 1961.

[8]
Barnet and Muller, *op.cit.*, pp. 111–12.

[9]
ibid., p. 93.

[10]
The experience of Allende's Chile, however, tells something of what happens when political developments take place against the interests of the corporations. The detailed attempts by ITT (and the CIA) to bring down Allende's government is one part of the story. Another is the plans laid by Kennecott Copper in anticipation of uncompensated nationalisation. Prior to Allende's election the company negotiated large loans and sold copper futures on the international finance and commodity markets. To quote their vice president for Chilean operations (Robert Haldeman): 'the aim of these arrangements is to ensure that nobody expropriates Kennecott without upsetting relations to customers, creditors, and governments in three continents.'

Chapter 2
The Old Vickers: The Government's Gunsmith

[1]
Vickers certainly did well out of its 'special relationship' with the government, and when these contracts were not taking up the Company's full capacity, it sold arms to the governments of Germany, Italy and Japan! In the mid 1930s for example, Vickers was inserting full page advertisements of field guns and tanks in German military journals. At around the same time the US Ambassador to Berlin was noting in his diary that 'Armstrong Vickers, the great British armament concern had negotiated a sale of war material here' and later that 'a British woman, connected with Hitler's inner group, was here to sell war equipment for Armstrong Vickers'. See Fenner Brockway, and R Mullay, *Death Pays a Dividend*, London, Gollancz Left Book Club 1947, chapters 6 and 7. In all of this, the payment of bribes to potential purchasers became an established fact of business. As one commentator puts it, 'the connection between arms and bribes was specially ominous, not only because of the danger of the product but because of the scope for expanding the market. The Vickers company . . . contended that the aggressive selling of arms did not increase the total sum spent on armaments . . . But other evidence, then and later,

has suggested that arms bribes were able to stimulate orders which might otherwise never have been made.' A Sampson, *The Arms Bazaar*, New York, Viking 1977, p. 55.

[2]
It is instructive here to compare the history of Vickers with that of the German arms manufacturer – Krupps. Krupps was forced to end arms production and, under strict state control and massive American funding, was transformed into a new powerful commercial empire. Vickers in contrast lingered on in the arms business. Its break with the past was made reluctantly and under the growing pressure of international competition. It has survived through diversification into light engineering and in Europe cannot challenge the capital intensive power of the German and Italian heavy engineering firms.

[3]
The material for much of this section is taken from the 'official' history of Vickers: J D Scott, *Vickers: A History*, London, Weidenfeld & Nicolson 1962.

[4]
In 1971, and after some rationalisation, Vickers had no less than 15 operating divisions at its main engineering works at Crayford, Swindon and Tyneside.

[5]
Graham Turner, *Business in Britain*, Harmondsworth, Penguin 1971.

Chapter 3
Shake-Up

[1]
G Turner, *Business in Britain*, Harmondsworth, Penguin 1971.
Turner's opinion was later supported as David Rowland the 27 year old tycoon started building up a stake in Vickers. By the end of 1973 his William Hudson Group had a 25 per cent shareholding. This led to much speculation about a take-over, and a lot of concern about Vickers defence interests falling into 'irresponsible and foreign hands' (Rowlands had business interests outside the UK). After a year or so of such high drama the press announced that 'To loud sighs of relief from the Vickers Millbank Tower block, William Hudson, quoted company of 28 year old David Rowland, has unloaded its 23.86 per cent interest in the engineering giant.' *The Newcastle Journal*, 7 August 1974.

[2]
By South African standards, Vickers is by no means the worst of the many companies which go out there in search of cheap labour. But

their statement to the Department of Trade that 'Vickers has a definite policy of no differentials in the rates paid as between European and others', is hypocritical and misleading. In 1973 Vickers employed a workforce of 275 (it has grown considerably since then with the Michell Bearing subsidiary set up in 1976). In only *three* cases did *coloured* workers have the same job as white workers (and even in one of these cases whites have a salary of *280 rands* a month and coloured *65*). In *no* case do *black* workers have the same job as white workers.

Chapter 4
The Helping Hand of the State

1

In writing about these handouts, and the role they have played in the restructuring of the Vickers company, we come up against the problem of business secrecy. Until amended by Tony Benn, the Industry Act made no provision for the public disclosure of information relating to the distribution of state aid. You might think that a government grant would show up easily in the company's balance sheet. But this is to underestimate the miasma of company accounting. The fact is that it is very difficult (even now) for trade unionists to get detailed information on the amount of state aid which goes to the company they work for.

2

At this point it is important to mention that the shop stewards and workers at Water Lane resisted the closure. For quite rational (and not 'old fashioned' or 'sentimental') reasons they felt that the plant could and should have been developed. They petitioned the government for aid and lobbied parliament. All to no effect.

3

In this deal, and the others, the close relationship which Vickers has had with government departments over the years has been of considerable significance. Vickers share their Headquarters at Millbank Tower with the NEDC. Their chairman and managing director were both prominent in the state sector. Since the war (and the break in the old 'service relationship') the company – probably more than any other – has been involved in repeated negotiations and discussions over nationalisation, denationalisation and compensation. Such is the social fabric of the new state.

4

The commercial yards do not figure at all in the manipulations that took place over the naval yards. Their position in the world market was extremely vulnerable and compensation was the most that owners of commercial yards could hope for.

Chapter 5
Taken Over

[1]
The metal decorating press, which was also produced at Water Lane, was eventually located at the Gateshead factory. This tendency to concentrate the production of a particular product at a particular plant was repeated throughout Vickers as management became more 'profit conscious'. Hydraulics were concentrated at South Marston, and the Weymouth plant closed down; armaments were based at Elswick at the cost of streamlining at Crayford and so on.

[2]
It seems clear that Crabtree – the firm that existed prior to Vickers' takeover – would have been forced to take these risks. While Vickers Ltd. spreads its investment throughout the wide number of options available to it, Crabtrees would have had to invest in the Water Lane plant – whatever the consequences.

[3]
It also points to the limits of plant (or locally) based trade union organisation. At Water Lane the only thing that the workers and their shop stewards were able to control and bargain over was the level of their redundancy payments.

Chapter 7
Developed

[1]
This division of Vickers Ltd. obtains orders, does all the design work, and then sub-contracts the production work to other companies, thereby securing profits with the maximum of overheads.

Chapter 8
The Paradox of Modernisation

[1]
E Christensen, *Automation*, London, Labour Research Department 1968, pp. 10–11.

[2]
Dan Sharpe, 'Computer numerical control as applied to machine tools', *Journal* (AUEW), May 1978.

[3]
H Braverman, *Labour and Monopoly Capital*, London Monthly Review Press 1975, p. 199.

[4]
M Cooley, 'Contradictions of science and technology in the productive process', in Hilary Rose and Steven Rose, eds., *The Political Economy of Science*, London, Macmillan 1976, p. 77.

[5]
Quoted in *Machine Tool Report*, Newcastle upon Tyne, Trade Union Studies Information Unit 1978, pp. 45–46 (available from TUSIU Southend, Fernwood Road, Newcastle 2).

[6]
Technological Change and Employment, ASTMS discussion paper 78.

[7]
Much of the information in the section is based upon the research conducted by the Benwell CDP; this is published in the following reports: (1) *Storing up Trouble*; (2) *Permanent Unemployment*; (3) *Regional Capitalism*; (4) *The Making of a Ruling Class*; (5) *Summary Report of Benwell CDP*; all published by Benwell CDP 1978 and available from Publications, 87 Adelaide Terrace, Newcastle 4.

[8]
Peter Ambrose and Bob Colenutt, *The Property Machine* Penguin 1975, p. 58.

Chapter 9
Why Should they Want to Meet?

[1]
During 1978 18 of Vickers' plants and their various shop stewards committees were contacted and the convenors asked to fill in a questionnaire. This has aimed at providing 'basic' information on each of the plants – number of people employed, kinds of technology and technological changes etc. – and also to find out what attitude the shop stewards committees adopted toward the national combine committee. This chapter is based upon these replies.

Chapter 10
The Making of the Combine

[1]
In the 1950s a strike took place on the night shift at the Elswick works which won the support of both the Tyneside factories. The night shift workers were required to work a short fifth shift on a Friday: they wanted to do away with this, and reduce the length of the working week. Their successful action ('Moonlight rebels win' headlined in the *Evening Chronicle*) was one of the first examples of successful joint plant action within the company.

[2]
The people who were delegated to seek support from other workers organisations in the area found this to be the most significant aspect of the strike – both from a trade union point of view and personally: 'I found that I had to talk with people, engage in conversation and explain things in a way I had never done before. I've never been very good at conversation . . . but going around to meetings, explaining our case, I've learned to talk to people. It has changed me quite a bit.'

[3]
The organisation of this committee was assisted financially by the Community Development Project (CDP) on Tyneside. The North East Committee also benefits from the research and clerical assistance provided by the Benwell CDP.

Chapter 11
The Problem of Unity

[1]
If the constitution and structure of the AUEW raises problems for the development of combine committees with any degree of autonomy, it might be argued that a union like the TGWU (where the independence of the district is replaced by a trade group structure which is established at the local and national level) might be more adaptable to such a re-organisation. To an extent this is true, and the successes which combine committee organisations have achieved in companies like Ford, Dunlop, Shell and to a lesser extent in ICI have been helped by the use of the trade group structure of the TGWU. However they did not achieve this without a struggle! In the 1930s, for example, the combine committee organised by the London busmen was savagely attacked by the TGWU Executive and its leaders expelled from the union. The experience of the dockers has been similar, and at both Dunlop and Ford combine committees were forced to develop outside of the union in the 1950s and 1960s.

Chapter 12
The Organisation of A Combine Committee

[1]
It is this inability to *enforce* decisions taken at combine meetings which has been a long standing problem for all combine committee organisations. The inability is often accepted and, by many, seen to be the way things should be anyway. However it is always a source of

irritation when decisions agreed at combine level, and supported by plant delegates, are not carried through at plant level. Combine committees have broken up (or at least, suffered serious set backs) as a consequence of such disagreements. The combine at Vickers experienced such a problem over the pensions issues where the agreement to opt out of the new company scheme was not backed in every affiliated plant.

[2]

Interestingly these steps mirror the steps taken in the early formation of trade unions with their respective district, regional and national committee structures. The extent to which past practices is used as a guide to new areas of action was made clear during the strike at Scotswood in 1977. That strike was (as we have noted) organised extremely efficiently and with a clearly thought out pattern. However the shop stewards did not notify plants affiliated to the national combine of their strike. At the Bridge Hotel meeting the Scotswood spokesman observed that 'we don't need to go running to them at this time. We will see if we can sort it out ourselves here first'. At the next meeting of the combine (which met the week after the strike ended) other delegates while warmly congratulating the Scotswood strikers, criticised the lack of contact – particularly because of the help that could have been offered in blacking work. The criticism was accepted by all north eastern delegates and the principle established that details on disputes should automatically be communicated throughout the plants in the combine.

[3]
H Friedman, 'Multi-plant working and trade union organisation', *Studies for Trade Unionists*, volume 2 number 8, December 1976, p. 20.

[4]
ibid., p. 7.

Chapter 13
Regulating Labour

[1]
This, along with the company songs and loyal workforces has been well publicised in Britain. However little has been said about the Japanese workers' experience of highly paced work and the high accident rate, or the severe economic threat which accompanies the sack. See for example *Nissan: Hell's Battlefield*, Solidarity Motor Bulletin (available from Solidarity, 123 Latham Road, London E6).

2
Don Roy, 'Fear stuff, sweet stuff, and evil stuff: management defences
against unionisation in the south' (mimeo).

3
Their flexibility is made clear by the enthusiasm with which they now
approach the project of production in Eastern Europe and China.
Vickers, for example has recently welcomed (and taken up) the
prospect of trading with China.

4
Work in America, Report of a Special Task Force to the Secretary
of Health, Education and Welfare, Cambridge, Mass., MIT Press
1973.

5
Quoted in *Big Business and Politics*, London, Labour Research
Department 1974.

Chapter 14
An Alternative Future?

1
G D H Cole, to B Pribicevic, *The Shop Stewards' Movement and
Workers' Control, 1910–1922*, London, Blackwell 1959.

2
M Cooley, 'Lucas: the right to *useful* work', *Workers' Control Bulletin*,
1978, no. 3, p. 3.

3
The Vickers combine committee invited Bob Cryer MP, a left wing
junior minister at the Department of Industry, to speak at one of its
weekend conferences. He concentrated upon the difficulties which big
business and the civil service put in the way of radical reform. He was
listened to sympathetically and delegates noted facts on the support
which the Labour government gave to big business. However the logic
of the question 'If it's like you say it is – what's the point of you being
there?' was inescapable.

4
This report is included in K Coates, ed., *The Right to Useful Work*,
Nottingham Spokesman Books 1978.

5
The fact that a good deal of what is being compensated for was built
with government assistance leads some people to ask: 'Why should
Vickers be paid anything at all?'

6
Quoted in *What Happened At Speke?* TGWU, Liverpool 1978
(available from 38 Caldwell Road, Allerton, Liverpool 19).

7
The issue of ownership also raises the issue of control over the savings
of workers themselves in pension funds, insurance companies and
building societies. The complete lack of democratic control over these
financial institutions on which workers depend led one steward to
reflect that 'Basically we're not better off as far as control goes to the
days when Armstrong was not only our employer but also our
landlord, and had power over us in retirement and sickness. We are
still oppressed in all these spheres.'

Index

167, 169–70; control of, 17, 18, 21, 59, 70, 186; flexibility of, 153, 176; significance of, 9, 10, 13, 16–17; *see also* Vickers, Management

National Coal Board, 33
Nationalisation, 49, 180–1, 191; *see also* Vickers
N.E.B., 181–2
N.E.D.C., 33, 198
Newcastle on Tyne, 9, 25, 42, 73, 74; city council, 101, 102; run-down, 73, 102–4, 123
N.G.A., 146
North Sea Oil, 56, 57
Norton, Walter, 47, 48

Office machinery, *see* Vickers

Parsons, C. A., 80
Participation, 59–62, 170–1, 188; *see also* Chrysler, I.C.I.
Pensions, *see* Vickers
Pearce, Dick, 144
Plessey, 28
Prais, S. J., 195
Printing News, 69
Profit, 15, 20–1, 25–7, 29, 31–2, 36, 43, 46–8, 50–1, 57, 69–70, 82, 104, 118, 176–7, 179, 183, 191; *see also* Multi-national corporations, Workers' plans

Quango, 10

Redundancy, 61, 71, 76, 86, 183–4; *see also* Vickers
Redundancy Payments Act, 84
Remmers, H. L., 195
'Revolutionary Capitalism', *see* Lonrho
Rowe Brothers, 65
Rowan, Leslie, 34
Robens, Alfred Lord, 10, 38, 49, 74, 89, 124; life history, 32–3; view of the world, 62, 92, 97, 162, 166, 167–8
Rolls Royce, 36, 44
Roneo, *see* Vickers
Rotary presses, 67, 68
Roy, Don, 203
Royal Commission on Trade Unions and Employers' Association, 33

Royal Society, 99

St. Regis International, 33
Sampson, A., 195
Scanlon, Lord Hugh, *see* AUEW
Scotswood Works, *see* Vickers
Scott, J., 28, 75, 76, 197
Senkes, P., 93
Shawcross, Hartley, 10
Sharpe, Dan, 94, 95, 100, 199
Shipbuilding industry, 49, 51
Shop Floor Voice, 116, 117, 119, 125, 156–7
Shop stewards committees (Vickers): Barrow, 52–3; Crabtree, 68–70, 98, 115–6, 121–3, 135, 155, 163; Elswick, 77–9, 138–41, 143, 163, 165, 180; Hastie Brothers, 48–9, 175; KTM, 48, 94–5, 140, 164–5; Roneo, 63–6, 131, 140, 142; Scotswood, 74–6, 80–2, 138, 140, 165; Slingsby Sail-planes, 89–93, 164; South Marston, 82–4, 100–1, 131–2, 163, 180
Shop steward combine committees, 11–12, 97, 106, 159, 171, 175, 192, 201; at Vickers, 114; information, 109–10, 117–8, 123, 127, 157; investment plans, 109, 158, 179, 186–8; isolation of plants, 110–11; membership, 126–7, 129–30, 155; need for combine, 107–8, 115, 121, 151, 159; official union attitude, 146–50; strikes, 121–2, 123–6, 131, 200–1, 202; structure of committee, 110, 120–1, 127–8, 152, 156, 202; relationship to company, 168–9
Silicone chip, *see* Automation
Slingsby Sailplanes, *see* Vickers
Skinner, Denis, 48
Solidarity, 81, 121–2, 127, 129, 131–2, 135, 141, 144; *see also* Shop steward combine committees
South Africa, 8, 42, 43
South Marston, *see* Vickers
Standard Telephone and Cables Ltd., 74, 99
State: and big business, 22–4; and participation, 171–2; and socialism, 180–2, 191; *see also* Vickers
Steel industry, 29, 34, 49